THE BOWMEN OF ENGLAND

The Bowmen of England

Donald Featherstone

NEW ENGLISH LIBRARY
TIMES MIRROR

First published in Great Britain by Jarrolds Ltd., 1967
© Donald Featherstone 1967

*

FIRST NEL PAPERBACK EDITION OCTOBER 1973

*

NEL Books are published by
New English Library Limited from Barnard's Inn, Holborn, London, E.C.1.
Made and printed in Great Britain by Hunt Barnard Printing Ltd., Aylesbury, Bucks.

45001626 9

Contents

Author's Introduction

At some time in their history nearly every race on earth has used the bow and arrow, but nowhere did they reach the pitch of skill and perfection as in England during the fourteenth and fifteenth centuries. In that period the English bowman dominated the wars of Europe as no comparable force has ever done since.

It was a time when England was a young nation, feeling her feet and still a little unsteady. The triple victories of Crécy, Poitiers and Agincourt stoked up the fires of national consciousness to forge a pride that has never left these shores. Directed by brilliant, brave and far-seeing captains, the English army did not lose a major battle between Morlaix in 1342 and Patay in 1429. The best professional fighting man of his day, the English yeoman, and his longbow were the most significant single factor that changed all the old traditions and concepts of mediaeval fighting and warfare.

The English archer was not a peasant to be lorded over by the higher born and arrogant of the land; he was a freeman, a respected yeoman possessing a proud and dignified status. He exchanged his exceptional skill and talents with the six-foot yew stave for specified pay and terms of military service. That he was a powerful, muscular man is obvious – only the biggest and the strongest of men could pull a hundred pounds and draw a full clothyard shaft to their ear. His background encouraged him to show initiative and resource, so that, when the occasion demanded, he would drop his bow and nimbly lay to with sword, axe and the murderous five-foot maule or mallet.

The successors of the English archer fought with Marlborough at Blenheim, Wolfe at Quebec, Clive at Plassey and with Wellington in the Peninsula. Their bones also salted the Sudanese sands and whitened on the rugged hills of India's north-west frontier; they amazed the Germans at Mons with their rapid rifle-fire and built up a reputation for dogged tenacity amidst adversity in two world wars. In the beginning the longbow brought the first immortal fame to the common soldier who might otherwise have hardly rated a mention in the history books.

Whether the longbow really altered the course of history is debatable, nor can it be claimed that the English archer contributed towards the foundation of the British Empire. But it cannot be denied that his skill and courage may well have discouraged other, more powerful, nations from attempting to add England to their empires.

In writing of Crécy, Poitiers and Agincourt one is writing of the Hundred Years War, of Edward, the Black Prince, and Henry V, but, more than that, one must write the history of the English archer, because without him, and the tactics built around him, none of the victories in France during that mediaeval period would have been possible.

It might well be claimed that historians have engaged in numerous and fierce controversies over battle sites, numbers engaged and casualties, and that these points of disagreement are not reflected in the pages of this book. To this point it is possible to give a number of valid reasons. In the first place it is intended that this should be the story of a man and his weapon – everything else is a background to that personalised account. Secondly, a considerable number of sources and authorities were consulted and studied during the preparation of this manuscript; many differed but none appeared to the author to improve upon or supplant the excellent reasoning of the late Lieutenant-Colonel A. H. Burne in his books on the Crécy and Agincourt wars. Therefore, much that is written and stated as fact in this book is so recorded because the author is convinced that it happened in that way – in the manner described by Colonel Burne and which requires no argument or discussion.

Further inspiration was gained from A. Conan Doyle's book *The White Company* – this most fascinating and enjoyable reading provided the initial impetus to put words on paper in praise of that truly English character and his weapon – the bowman. I am grateful to John Murray (Publishers) Ltd. of London for their unhesitating permission to quote from this wonderful book.

This is perhaps the sixth book that I have written with the invaluable aid of Southampton Public Library. Volumes long since out of print have been sought and borrowed from other libraries by Bob Corlett and Bill Graham, to whom I owe a great deal.

Donald Featherstone

Southampton

Prologue

It was a good position to hold. From the top of the small hill the archers gazed around them, noting with professional eyes its defensive merits – they liked the long and gradual slope that dropped away in their front, remarked that its tangled undergrowth and stony surface would handicap the horses. The patches of soggy marshland on either flank formed a comforting guard and there was a nice convenient wood right behind them to hold the baggage-train. Yes, it had been well chosen.

Amid the bustle and preparation that ensued on all sides, the bowmen appeared calm and confident as they methodically new-strung their bows and made sure that they were firm at the nocks. From his steel skull-cap each archer removed a carefully coiled bowstring, unrolling it gently so as not to twist it more or less than the natural twist already in it. The bow end was placed against the inside of the left foot to prevent it digging into the ground, the handle grasped with the left hand so that the bow sloped away to the right, with the back uppermost. Then the top loop of the string was slipped over the upper end of the bow and allowed to drop a few inches down the stave; the lower loop put safely home in the bottom nock on the bow. Against the back of the bow, a few inches from the top, each bowman placed the palm of a horny hand, with the first finger and thumb on either side of the string about halfway down the loop, taking care that no finger got round the underside of the bow or between the string and bow. Next, he pulled on the handle with his left hand and pushed at the top with the right, sliding the right hand and the loop of the string upwards until the loop slipped into the nock. With a studied and practised nonchalance he relaxed gradually, just in case the bottom loop had slipped out of place.

Bows ready for action, the peeled six-foot poles, roughly sharpened at each end, were picked from the ground where they had been dropped by each man when they halted. Using daggers, holes were dug in front of them, and one end of the pole dropped into the small pit. Mauls were then used to hammer home the stakes, the pointed ends being re-sharpened when the poles were firm. In a short time there was a barrier of threatening stakes pointing obliquely upwards, in a solid fence that undulated with the rise and fall of ground across the front of the position.

Whilst the archers worked, their officers and file-leaders moved among them, giving an instruction here, a word of advice there. The senior of the master bowmen raised his voice so that those around him could hear:

'Now listen, me lads! Make sure you've got all you need . . . a bracer on your left hand, a shooting glove on your right . . . have your wax handy too. Remember, bend your bow well . . . nock your stave properly and lock your string well!'

'My old dad told me them things afore I was knee-high to him!'

A roar of laughter greeted the sally, growled out by a tanned and grizzled veteran, looking up from checking string-height by his own 'fist-mele'. The master bowman glowered at him; turning away he muttered:

'I'll remember you . . . if we get out of this alive!'

One of the older bowmen called after him:

'Don't pay him no heed, Master Robin! He's a good lad at heart! Remember him an' his mates at Crécy? Little Hal Watridge, and Perkin of Winchester . . . an' Wat Purkiss who brought down the big plumed lord? God in heaven . . . they were men we won't see the like of no more! I dare say they could beat any we got here at long butts or short, hoyles, rounds or rovers!'

A trumpet shrilled loud and clear above the clamour. Still buckling armour and testing weapons, the soldiers flowed into familiar formations, to stand at ease. The archers fell into four lines with under-officers and file-leaders in front and on the flanks; in a ripple of movement that ran down their ranks they removed the skull-caps and bowed their heads. All men stood silent, alone with their thoughts, as their leaders harshly muttered a prayer; then in a rustling monotone all repeated the Pater, the Ave and the Credo. The men-at-arms, in their dull, leaden-hued armour, the ruddy visages, craggy features and hard bearded faces joined together in a sudden hush; some of the men drew amulets and relics from their tunics, to be kissed and carefully replaced. The last 'Amen', deep and resonant, had barely rolled through the still air when the reverent silence was broken by the distant squeal of trumpets, the deep rolling of drums, backed by the dull monotone of footsteps and many thousands of voices.

All eyes turned towards the crest of the ridge, three-quarters of a mile distant across the valley, that lay at the foot of their own hill; it was now topped with countless lance pennons, glittering steel points, colourful surcoats and waving plumes.

'It's them . . . 'ere they are, lads!'

'Jist got 'ere in time, din' we?'

They stood in silence, watching the enemy mass in their thousands, saw their formations ripple and shudder as the impatient knights tried to fight their way to the front, jealous of any others who might take from them the honour of opening the battle. In spite of the confidence that they felt, many of the English archers and men-at-arms were unable to prevent their eyes from travelling quickly over their own small force and comparing it with that of the enemy – at least four times as numerous. By now they were close enough to be individually distinguished, but still just out of bowshot. In response to murmured orders, short arrows were nocked to perhaps a thousand bowstrings, to be loosed to fall far short of the opposing army in an effort to encourage it to come closer. The challenge was accepted and now the battle was about to begin in earnest.

'Think they're within range?'

'Dunno . . . it's near twenty score paces. Still, we oughter be able to notch a mark at that distance. Come on, Perkin, Watkin of Fareham and Big John . . . let's show 'em they've got English bowmen to deal with!'

'I'll take the lord with the white-and-red plume.'

'An' I him with the gold headpiece!'

From his stock of two dozen bodkin-pointed arrows planted in the ground before him, each archer drew one, nocked it, bent his bow, and, on the order: 'Loose!', let it fly with thousands of others up, up into the air above the approaching enemy. It climbed swiftly with a soul-shrivelling howl and whip, like a gale in the tops of tall trees. As the enemy fearfully gazed upwards to watch them, the shafts turned, to become a swarm of black specks against the sky, plummeting down towards them. Then, together with a hundred others, the knights wearing the red-and-white plume and the gold headpiece crashed to the ground in a clanking, tumbling heap of horses and men.

'Higher, Wat, higher!'

'Put thy body into it, Will!'

'Forget not the wind, Arnold!'

On all sides rose a muttered chorus of advice: shrewd pro-

11

fessional comments on their craft of skilfully using a stave of wood and a string such as they had never been used before. Above all could be heard the sharp twanging of the strings, the hiss and howl of the shafts, mingled with orders and advice from the officers and the master bowman:

'Draw your arrow!'

'Nick your arrow!'

'Shoot wholly together!'

None of the enemy cavalry got closer to them than fifty yards; most remained in their crumpled heaps on the muddy, blood-stained and scuffled slope of the hill. The archers ceased firing and rested on their bows, exultantly talking among themselves.

'I've got thirteen arrows left . . . an' I'll sink every one of 'em in French flesh or my name ain't what it is!'

'Dickon, did ye see the black-armoured lord? I took both him and his horse with but one shaft!'

The enemy grouped, massed into an even larger formation than the first; the trumpets sounded, the horses were spurred into a trot and then cumbrously they lurched upwards towards the English position once again. The bowmen were ready, feet firmly planted, sleeves rolled back to give free play to their arms, long yellow bow-staves held out in front of them, they waited in the four-deep harrow formation which gave strength to their array and permitted every man to draw his arrow freely without harm to the men in front of him. Some of the bowmen threw light tufts of grass into the air to gauge the wind force; hoarse whispers ran down the ranks from the file-leaders:

'Hold your arrows! Don't loose outside fifteen score paces We'll need all our shafts before we've beaten this lot!'

'Don't undershoot, lads! Better to hit a man in their rear than have your shaft feather in the earth!'

'Loose quick and sharp when they get near.'

The master bowman, passing behind, heard this last remark; he quickly answered:

'Keep your eye to the string and the string to the shaft and it will find its mark!'

The glittering enemy squadrons tossed and heaved, they surged forward, trotting, now cantering, then galloping – the whole vast array was hurtling forward, line after line, the air full of the thunder of their hooves and the ground shaking. The valley was choked with the rushing torrent of steel, topped by waving plumes, slanting lances and fluttering pennons. On they swept over the level and then up the slope, to be met with a blinding drift of English arrows that brought down whole ranks in a whirl of mad confusion; horses plunging and kicking, bewildered and stunned men rising or wallowing like upturned turtles in their heavy armour. But new lines forced their way through the fallen, crushing and riding down wounded men and horses; spurring through the gaps in the mounds of dead, new lines of horsemen urged themselves up the slope.

On all sides could be heard the shrill, stern, short orders of the master bowmen and file-leaders; the air was filled with the keen twanging of their bowstrings and the swish, howl and patter of their shafts.

'Right between the eyes, by heavens! But I meant it for his throat!'

'Now . . . who's next? Ah, the lord with the leopard on his surcoat!'

'That's it! To the inch!'

'Good shot for you, Arnold!'

'Thank 'ee. When my eye is in I'm better at rovers than at long butts or hoyles!'

'Loose gently! Loose gently, lads! Don't pluck with the drawing hand! 'Tis a trick that has marred many a good bowman!'

Across the foot of their hill a wall of struggling men and horses had built up, which grew higher as fresh men and horses added to it. Led by a big knight on a grey destrier, a body of the enemy pushed resolutely onward until they reached the English line. As they forced their way through the pointed stakes, their leader fell within a spear-length of the English position, the feathers of arrows thrusting out from every crevice and joint of his armour.

The battle was now a fierce, tumbling hand-to-hand conflict that surged and flowed in and around the now beaten-down stakes in front of the English position. Their arrows gone, the archers drew swords, clutched axes or fearsome five-foot mauls and nimbly ran to the outskirts of the clanging, roaring, desperate melee. Lightly creeping under horses' bellies, dancing around ponderous, heavily armoured men-at-arms, they slashed, stabbed, clubbed and hewed until they were as bloody as the red-mottled heap amidst which they fought. Slowly, remorselessly, the enemy were forced back down the hill; they fought fiercely, but here and there wounded and faint-hearted men lurched from the tangled mob and made their struggling way down the hill, to be chased and fallen upon by the fast-moving archers like dogs on a rabbit. Once down, the heavily armoured men were helpless and easy prey to the judiciously inserted long knife through a crevice or

13

joint in their armour. The enemy wavered, trembled, and then turned and fled on all sides.

'They run!'

' 'Tis a trick!'

'Nay, you fool! They're beaten . . . we've won!'

'Thank God.'

'Hooray for England, Edward and St. George!'

PART ONE

THE BIRTH OF THE BOW

1

The Earliest Days

The shooting of arrows with a bow is undoubtedly one of the oldest of the arts still practised today. For thousands of years the simple bow held its own as a long-distance weapon; it was the most widely used and generally dispersed of all weapons, spreading from nations whose history is still bound in the past all over the world. Man's constant companion from the earliest days until the sixteenth century, it was probably his first invention of a device in which energy can be accumulated slowly, stored temporarily and released suddenly with control and direction, leading to great accuracy of projection over two or three hundred yards. Claimed to rank in importance as a cultural advance with the development of speech and the discovery of the art of making fire, the bow and arrow goes back at least 30,000 years.

It is not hard to imagine the emancipation brought about by the bow and arrow. Man had lived for thousands of years in peril of his life and livelihood, having to kill his food and his enemies with his bare hands, or, at best, with crude extensions to his hands such as stone hammers and axes. To live he had to be a fast mover, get in close and strike quickly with little time to ensure that his blow fell in a lethal place on his quick and active quarry. With the coming of the bow he had leisure to aim carefully at a safe distance from his target; his power to kill depended no longer on his physical strength alone; he was the equal of his fellows, no matter how big and strong they might be.

Although nearly every race on earth used the bow at some time, nowhere did the art and skill of archery reach such a pitch of development as in the English longbowman of the thirteenth, fourteenth and early fifteenth centuries. During those years packed ranks of English archers dominated the wars of Europe as no comparable force has ever done since. The mere sight of them was enough to strike the fear of God into an enemy who, if he did not retreat or keep his distance, was almost certainly slaughtered. Somehow the enemy never learned this. French, Irish and Scots –

each of them lost thousands of their youth and nobility to the laconic English bowman. But the English longbow, when it played havoc with the Scots, was no new weapon, nor was its origin English. Bows had been known from prehistoric times and were used at the Battle of Hastings and in the Crusades, but these were not true longbows unless they were drawn to the ear and not merely to the breast. In England, as all over the Continent, the 'short' bow was held in little esteem, not even being mentioned in Henry II's Assize of Arms in 1181.

It is impossible to trace the actual origin of the longbow, but there is good evidence that it was in use in South Wales during the second half of the twelfth century. Giraldus Cambrensis speaks repeatedly of the men of Gwent and Morganwg as excelling all others in the practice of archery; he gives evidence too of the effects of their shooting. At the siege of Abergavenny in 1182 the Welsh arrows penetrated an oak door said to be at least four inches thick. They were allowed to remain there as a curiosity and Gerald himself saw them six years later, in 1188, when he passed the castle, their iron points just showing on the inner side of the door. During the same period a knight of William de Braose was hit by one which went through the skirt of his hauberk, his mail hose, his thigh and through the leather and wood of his saddle and into his horse; when he swerved round another arrow pinned him in the same way by the other leg!

'What more could a bolt from a balista have done?' asked Gerald. Describing the bows of Gwent, he says: 'They are made neither of horn, ash nor yew but of elm; ugly, unfinished-looking weapons, but astonishingly stiff, large and strong, and equally capable of use for long or short shooting.'

These were the bows, in the hands of the South Welsh bowmen, which were used in the Norman invasion of Ireland in 1171. The Normans had learned of the power of the Welsh shafts and dreaded them; William de Brensa, having convened a meeting of the principal chiefs of South Wales at Abergavenny Castle some years previously, made them purchase their liberty by swearing they would not in future allow any of their followers to travel armed with the bow. '*Ne quis gladium ferret vistor vel arcum.*' In 1120 Henry II undertook an expedition into Wales, being opposed by Meredith ap Blethyn. Near the confines of Powys some young Welsh archers enfiladed the English in a woody pass, one arrow glancing off the King's breastplate, greatly alarming him. On another occasion, whilst the English were attempting to force a bridge, the King was recognised and a Welsh archer aimed at him.

Seeing this, a Norman baron, Hubert de St Clare, Constable of Colchester, threw himself forward and was killed when the arrow pierced his breast. The Welsh had found it necessary to hunt and fight at greater distances than usual in their mountainous country and so had increased the size and thickness of their bows to obtain more power. They then found, their only timber being wych-elm, that to be reliable they had to be at least the height of the archer if he was fully to draw an arrow suited to his stature.

Writing of the Normans' Irish invasion, Gerald tells how the first contingent, under Robert Fitzstephen, sailed for Ireland with ninety mailed men-at-arms and 300 foot archers 'of the flower of the young men of Wales'. This combination of mounted men-at-arms and archers was found to be irresistible. Gerald noted its effectiveness; so, too, a century later, did Edward I in his Welsh wars. Twice the spearmen of Snowdonia went down before the archers from Gwent laced with horsemen, once at Orewin Bridge and then near Conway.

The longbow is about the simplest piece of mechanism imaginable, consisting of only a bowstave and string; it possessed three distinct advantages in that it was cheap to produce, had a fairly extensive range and provided rapidity of discharge. Such an elementary weapon was eminently suitable for use by peasant militia, for it had no complications of mechanism and no professional skill was needed. The English archer of the fourteenth century had about as little drill – apart from practice at the butts – as the Boer farmer did in 1899, but he took as kindly to his weapon as the Boer did to his rifle.

A landmark in the history of archery was reached in Henry III's Assize of Arms in 1251; that document commands that: '. . . all who own more than 40 or less than 100 schillings in law come bearing a sword and bow with arrows and a dagger.' Similarly, citizens with chattels worth more than nine marks and less than twenty are to be armed with bow, arrows and sword; there is a special clause providing that even poor men with less than this should bring bows and arrows, if they had them. Initially being the natural weapon of the yeoman for hunting (also of the outlaw and poacher) and of the common soldier, the bow was the ideal weapon for the purpose. It was beneath the dignity of noblemen, who hunted with sword, spear and hounds, to stalk and kill game in silence with an arrow, from a distance. Thus, wh n a feudal lord summoned his knights and barons to go to war, their lowest ranks, impressed peasants, bore the only weapon they possessed – the bow, although a shorter one at first.

But when the longbow came into its own, shooting with it was not the same pleasant pastime as using the shorter hunting bow; the longbow had a draw-weight of perhaps seventy-five pounds. With plans in mind for the Welsh longbow, Edward I confirmed Henry's Assize of Arms by the Statute of Winchester, making practice compulsory on Sundays and Holydays. On many a sandstone village church grooves can still be seen where archers sharpened their arrows after Mass, preparatory to doing butt practice. Other games, such as football, handball and cockfighting, were made illegal; direction of labour was introduced so that bowyers and fletchers could be compelled to reside where they were most needed, and there were many acts regulating the price of equipment. In the first half of the thirteenth century the bow appears to have been in greater vogue in the northern than in the western counties of England. The rather obvious theory that men from the woodland regions were proficient in bowmanship is substantiated by an attack made in the Weald during 1264–5 by De Montfort's archers on King Henry's marching columns. Then there is a writ issued in May 1266 ordering Roger de Leyburn to raise 500 archers in the Weald; in this writ from the Exchequer Accounts these archers are called 'WALLENSES, WALDENSES *et alii*' (Welsh foresters and others). Contemporary documents often speak of the obligation of various manors to provide the King with one or more archers . . . 'when he makes an expedition against the Welsh.' It is curious to note that even as late as 1281 Richard the Lionheart's preference for crossbowmen seems to have been maintained, the wages of its bearer being considerably more than those of the archer. In the pay-roll of the garrison of Rhuddlan Castle in 1281 it is noted that . . . 'paid to Geoffrey le Chamberlin for the wages of 12 crossbowmen, and 13 archers, for 24 days, £7 8s. Each crossbowman receiving by the day 4d. and each archer 2d.'

Oddly, when the Assize of Arms in 1181 organised English national forces, the bow did not appear in the list of national weapons, although it had been in full use for some time as such. It might well be that the authorities hesitated to recommend the keeping of a bow in every poor freeman's cottage because of the very strong temptation to employ it for poaching! Edward I altered this in 1285 when he re-enacted the Assize of Arms, redistributing the national force into new formations armed with new weapons. Archers were re-established by statute, although restricted to bows and bolts if they lived in the forest – the bolt being less deadly to the King's deer than their arrows. Edward I, like his grandson and great-grandson, was an able soldier, capable of devising new expedients in war. Unlike them, he also showed considerable strategical ability. This monarch, through his long experience in Welsh wars, introduced a scientific use of archery thus originating the longbow's rise to favour. But his methods had been foreshadowed more than half a century earlier – Henry I dismounted his knights and won at Tenchbriar (Tinchebrai) in 1106, against Robert of Normandy; he again was victorious at Breuville in 1125 in the same manner. But at Beaumont he added a company of archers who moved off to their left flank when the Norman cavalry came thundering down, to be overthrown with a shower of arrows. These archers must not be confused with those of a later date, but were probably copied (like the order of battle) from a Byzantine model. They taught the English the second of two most useful lessons – Henry had already discovered that dismounted knights could hold their own against the impetuous French knights; now he learned that a cavalry attack could be weakened, almost to annihilation, by volleys of archers.

Such knowledge, at a time when cavalry held absolute supremacy in war, was a secret of unfathomable value; a secret indeed which laid the foundations of England's very military power. Henry was evidently alive to the secret, and encouraged the practice of archery by ordaining that if any man should by accident slay another at the butts the misadventure should not be reckoned to him as a crime.

The year 1138 was memorable for the first of the many actions fought against the Scots – the Battle of the Standard was typical of many victories to come. The English knights fought on foot and, aided by archers, made havoc of the enemy. Dimly, through the mist of time, one can see already the germ of the later English infantry – in forthcoming centuries lances and bows gave way to pikes and muskets, but for five whole centuries the foot soldiers were compounded of two elements, offensive and defensive, until the invention of the bayonet slowly welded them into one. The French invented the mimic warfare known as the tournament which, not being a duel of man against man but essentially a contest of troop against troop, was a training for tactics, skill, discipline and leadership; victory turning mainly on skilful handling of the men and the preservation of compact order. Thus, by the blending of English foot soldiers and Norman cavalry, was laid earlier than in any other European country the foundation of an army wherein both branches took an equal share of work in the day of action.

The period between 1300 and 1500 saw the slow transition from mediaeval to modern world; a transition affecting the art of war as well as everything else. It can easily be claimed that the most significant single factor that changed all the old traditions and concepts of mediaeval fighting techniques was the development of the longbow in the hands of English peasants directed by brilliant and far-seeing leaders. It reduced war to two simple elements, one of which or both of which have to be employed to defeat an enemy – he must be overthrown either by shock or by missile-fire or by both in combination. The shock method means that success is achieved when one side bests another, often through superior numbers, in a hand-to-hand struggle. This method is materially affected also by the superiority of arms or the greater strength and skill with which they are wielded. The missile method means that the day is won by one side keeping up such a constant and deadly rain of missiles that the enemy are destroyed or driven back before they can come to close quarters; this method enables a smaller force to defeat a larger one. Both methods are capable of combinations of various arms and tactics, with countless variations and techniques.

In their simplest and most elementary forms the English archer and the Swiss pikeman represented these two basic methods of military efficiency. The former relied on his ability to beat the enemy by highly trained, skilled shooting of great accuracy; the latter by being able to present a solid column with a formidable hedge of spear-points surmounting it, so that it was possible to drive before them superior numbers of the enemy who were unable to withstand the crashing impact and steady pressure of the pikemen. The common factor was that both methods were triumphant against, and overthrew, the heavy, mail-clad horsemen who had for so long been masters of the battlefield. Because of the marked superiority of the two methods they were copied and emulated by those who had suffered from them; but neither was easy to accomplish and no one ever succeeded in becoming better than the originators.

And so the whole military system of the mediaeval period was torn asunder, to be profoundly modified and irrevocably altered. After the rise of the English archer the art of war took on a new and more serious complexion: it had been transformed from the rather glorious extension of the tournament that it had become into a bloody business requiring intelligence and the utmost wariness.

22

2

The Welsh Wars – late Thirteenth Century

By the last quarter of the thirteenth century archery had become a recognised military arm of great importance to England. The Royal Statutes compelled every person earning less than 100 pence per year to have in his possession a bow and arrows, officers being appointed by the Crown to see that all these weapons were in good order and ready for instant use. If the owners of the weapons lived within the confines of, or near to, the Royal Forests, an early conservation measure ruled that their arrows should be blunt ones. The archer was beginning to be recognised as a person of military importance, as can be seen from an ancient military ordinance:

'And in special, at the first moustre, every archere shall have his bowe and arrowes hole, that is to wytte, in arrowes xxx or xxiv at the least, headed and in a sheaf. And furthermore, that every archere do sweare that his bowe and arrowes be his own, or his mastyres or captaynes. And also that no man ones moustered and admitted as an archere, alter or change himself to any other condition, without the Kinge's special leave, upon payne of imprisonment.'

Poachers and outlaws in Sherwood Forest were offered a pardon on condition they served in the King's army as archers. This was not simply a general or meaningless pardon either; the offence for which each man was pardoned is specified, clear indication of the value put upon them. These criminals (like their descendants in Wellington's Peninsula army) amply vindicated England's fighting capacity by gaining a notable victory at Halidon Hill in 1333. When it is considered just how serious poaching was viewed in those days, the pardoning comes into its correct perspective. Brief examination and a speedy fate awaited the luckless Saxon who loved a buck's haunch more than he feared the penalties of the forest law, or whose wife and children's piteous pleading for food spurred him to venture forth with bow and arrow amid the trees. A caballistic verse reveals the suspicious circumstances that could bring summary justice to the unfortunate man:

> 'Dog draw,
> Stable stand,
> Black berond,
> Bloody hand.'

Thus is indicated the four evidences by which, according to the old feudal laws, a man was convicted of deer-stealing. The first relates to an offender caught in a forest, drawing after a deer with a hound in leash; the second to him caught with a bent bow ready to shoot; the third to bearing away the venison on his shoulders and the fourth to him merely found with hand stained with blood.

Edward the Confessor's Red Book contains the following caution:

'*Omnis homo abstest a venariis meis, super poenam vitae.*' (Let every man refrain from my hunting grounds on pain of death.)

A nearby tree would form a ready gallows, his own bowstring the halter by which they strangled him like a hound.

Realising that the necessary skill with the longbow could only be reached with constant and unremitting practice, the strictest means were taken to ensure that every able-bodied man got in his hours of practice shooting. Peers and churchmen were privileged by law, but no other persons, aliens excepted, could absent themselves from the public exercise ground without incurring what was then considered a serious penalty. So the independent franklin, the wealthy yeoman, the rude peasant and the unwashed artisan all congregated, distinction of rank lost sight of for the time, and adroitness alone giving title to superiority. The ancient public butts were so thronged with archers, particularly at holiday times, that they raked up the surrounding turf by the very arrows that missed, in such a manner that the grass would not grow again in the same spots. The continual tramping of feet as the bowmen circulated about the marks also contributed to destroy the turf and vegetation. In the vicinity of the large and populous towns the concourse must have been enormous and for this reason the archer used but a single arrow when practising. Besides the impossibility of getting in a second shot amid such confusion, he found it necessary to hurry away to the opposite butt in order to catch up his shaft before it was stolen or trodden under foot.

Notwithstanding all this activity, King Edward I complained

by letter to the Sheriff of London that archery had fallen into a grievous condition; he said that skill with the bow was put aside in favour of useless sports and commanded that hereinafter the Sheriff should see to it that such idle practices where abandoned and that leisure time upon holidays should be spent in the noble recreation of archery.

It fell to Edward III to reap the full benefit of English bowmanship, but his grandfather, seen complaining above, planted and fostered in such a way the seed. Even before his first Welsh war, in 1277 Edward showed his interest in the Welsh longbow; in that year a special force of 100 picked men of Macclesfield in the King's own lands, were purely archers unmixed with spearmen. They served from the first day of the war, which broke out later in that year, to the very last day at the then extraordinary wage of 3d. per day; whereas the other infantry came up only for short periods. The only other purely bow-armed force of this war came from Gwent and Crickhowell and that, too, served for a longer time than usual.

The early fourteenth century saw the evolution of a coherent military practice which used in a single tactical scheme the distinctive power of archery, the defensive solidarity of dismounted men-at-arms and, when necessary, the offensive power of mounted troops. Edward had discovered, or comprehended what was already apparent, first the virtues of archery in attack to break up a defensive infantry formation and, second, its power in defence when based on array of dismounted knights and men-at-arms. A beginning was made in the Welsh wars: at Orewin Bridge in 1282 and at Maes Maydog in 1295, the first against the men of Prince Llewelyn, who prepared to stand their ground in a defensive position. The English advanced against them, archers interposed with cavalry – the arrows inflicting sufficient loss on the Welsh troops to cause them to loosen their cohesion and fall into comparative disorder so that the cavalry were able to ride them down. In the second battle, near Conway, the Earl of Warwick used the same tactics. A contemporary report says:

'The Welsh on the earl's approach, set themselves fronting his force with exceeding long spears, which, being suddenly turned toward the earl and his company with their ends placed in the earth and their points upwards, broke the force of the English cavalry. But the earl well provided against them, by placing archers between his men-at-arms, so that by these missive weapons those who held the lances were put to rout.'

In later battles with the other hereditary enemy, the Scots, the effectiveness of combined archery and cavalry action against immobile infantry formations was shown. Such were the beginnings of the use of English infantry to be a power in war; the seventy years which followed the opening of Edward's Welsh wars saw striking developments both in military organisation and tactics. Both led to the same culmination – those English victories which astonished Europe in the opening stages of the Hundred Years War. It remained for Edward I in his later campaigns, and for his grandson Edward III, to get the English to become expert in the use of the longbow by practice, and to learn to act as a disciplined corps. Yet even after the Battle of Halidon Hill the English had no military reputation whatsoever. Jehan le Bel is quite explicit in showing that their triumph at Crécy came as a complete surprise to the whole of Continental Europe.

3

The Armies of the English and the French

In spite of having a population three or four times larger than that of England, France was never able, until the latter stages of the Hundred Years War, to put into the field an army capable of standing up to the English forces. There were a number of factors responsible for this, but mainly it can be laid down to superior English methods of recruitment, allied to the fact that they could command from time to time both Welsh and Irish troops; this was only slightly offset by bodies of Scots under French command. For the first part of the war, England, like France, constituted their army on a feudal basis, backed by the National Militia (the Fyrd). Edward III revolutionised this system by instituting a method of organisation that was certainly the most significant development in the history of the English army in the late Middle Ages. From the campaign of 1341 Edward III had replaced the old feudal levy with a system of written indentured contracts between the Crown and the captains of armed retinues, a method of raising paid professional soldiers for service in the field that was to remain until the end of the Hundred Years War.

By these means a commander contracted with the King to

provide a specified force for military service; the force generally being of all arms such as men-at-arms, mounted and foot archers and foot spearmen. The indenture laid down precisely the size and the composition of the force, its rates of pay, the place of assembly together with its obligations and privileges. The length of service varied, the shortest period being the traditional forty days and the longest time was normally one year, after which a man took his discharge or signed on again for a further period. The English army had lifted itself from the dragging chains of the feudal system to become a paid, professional short-service army in which the mounted noble and the yeoman archer served overseas at the King's wage. It was a highly trained and disciplined mercenary army; a soldier drawing regular pay for his services is more amenable to discipline than the man dependent on looting and plunder. Edward's army was the most powerful and highly trained force of its day.

France, on the other hand, never succeeded, or even tried, to rid herself of the feudal system of raising troops until the closing years of the war. Her army was the usual feudal host, composed of a heterogeneous collection of lords all claiming equality with the other, backed by jealous retainers – all subject to the slenderest control by the Constable of France. The old conceptions remained, infantry were scorned and the knights not only regarded themselves as the backbone of the army but considered that they *were* the army! The usual local levies produced ill-trained infantry who were strengthened by foreign mercenaries such as the Genoese crossbowmen, and occasionally aided by bodies of courageous Scots carrying on, in different fields, their perpetual struggle with the English. At the very beginning of the war Crécy proved the stock example of French disdain for any form of co-operation between aristocratic cavalry and all other despised arms, it was a lesson that France took nearly a century to learn.

In spite of the length of the war there were surprisingly little changes or developments in arms, armament or method of fighting, with the sole exception of artillery, which showed marked progress in power and effectiveness, and in armour, which gradually changed from mail to plate. In the matter of arms and armament the soldiers of both countries were not dissimilar. Both sides had men-at-arms (knights were men-at-arms but men-at-arms were not necessarily knights) armed similarly with sword, lance, dagger and sometimes battle-mace, helm, shield and spurs completing the equipage. The knight had three armed attendants, who might be pages to clean and polish his armour, help him in and out of it, hold his horse and assist him to mount; they also groomed the horse; then he had two mounted archers and one swordsman; the whole constituting a 'Lance'. He also had three or four horses, including two heavy chargers (destriers). Men-at-arms were covered in armour from top to toe (cap á pie), but as the development was in a stage of transition in the fourteenth century, it is difficult to describe their equipment with certainty. The increase in plate-armour reduced the mobility of the man-at-arms as it reduced the effectiveness of the arrow. They do not seem to have been great horsemen. It is recorded that sometimes they were tied to the saddle; but the horses were undoubtedly difficult to manoeuvre – the bits were too weak, the cumbrousness of the saddle and the weight of the armour were obstacles to good horsemanship. From the end of the thirteenth century the horses themselves wore defensive armour. To protect its head the horse wore a *chanfron*, whilst the neck was covered with a *crinet* with mail attachment. The front of the horse's body was protected by the *peytral*, its sides by the *flanchards* and its rear by the *crupper*. A strong horse had no difficulty in carrying this defensive covering which in the later stages of its development only weighed just over seventy pounds, including saddle and mail.

The shield gradually became obsolete owing to the effectiveness of plate-armour and its ineffectiveness against cannonballs. Briefly, armour improved slowly from about the middle of the thirteenth century when mail was worn, with a flat-topped barrel helm; then from about 1280 it was reinforced with plate and the helm was 'sugar-loaf'; from 1300 there was further plate reinforcement, and a visored helm (the great bascinet), and in the fifteenth century complete plate-armour was common – this was undoubtedly the finest period of armour.

There is plenty of evidence in the chronicles of the French wars that if men-at-arms, covered completely in plate, advanced against English bowmen without their too-vulnerable horses then they would stand at least some chance of coming to hand-strokes. When a body of fully armoured men-at-arms plodded with bent heads into the storm of arrows, however powerfully the shafts struck the hard, smooth, curved surfaces of the armour, they would glance off unless they found lodgement where plate overlapped plate. There were no exposed joints except for the weak spots at the shoulder where the spandlers met the armholes of the breastplate. Realising this, the English archers often fired at the face and throat, so that, when the man-at-arms unwarily lifted his visor or removed his gorget during a hot day, he often received a shaft in this most vulnerable spot. Chroniclers claim that few men who lifted their visors in battle ever lived to close them again! Later, at Towton during the Wars of the Roses, Lord de Clifford, faint with pain, heat and thirst, took off his gorget – instantly an arrow passed through his neck and killed him.

However, if the arrows did not penetrate the armour their effects were such as though they did, for the presence of archers in the field eventually compelled the French to advance on foot. Though plate-armour is not much heavier than mail, and is most flexibly jointed, it is not meant for marching in. The necessity of having to trudge a mile or more, often uphill or over ploughed land or through long grass and scrub (as at Mauron in 1352 and at Poitiers in 1356), and to fight at the end of it, was almost as devastating to the French men-at-arms as having his horse shot from under him. More often than not, he died in either case. It is most marked that in *all* the English victories during the Hundred Years War it was always the French who attacked and trudged up the hills in their armour. The English quietly stood about, waiting in their strong, carefully chosen defensive positions, perfectly fresh for combat when the exhausted Frenchmen came to grips with them.

And that was not all. In having to face the deadly shafts of the English longbowman the men-at-arms had to suffer the extremely bewildering and nerve-racking effect of the deadly missiles hissing and humming past them, smacking on their armour and ricocheting off it. Few soldiers have had to face arrows *and* musket-balls at the same time, but the evidence of those who have (in India with Clive) unanimously agree that the arrows were more demoralising than the balls.

When the French attacked on horse it was their practice to pack their men-at-arms into a close and solid mass; until the moment of action there was only sufficient space allowed for each horse to turn in its own ground. But for the actual attack ranks and files closed up as tightly as possible to maintain a compact array so that it was recorded than an apple thrown into the middle of attacking French knights would not have reached the ground. These methods played into the hands of the English archer, who, even if he was not always able completely to prevent the French attack striking home, was able so to decimate its ranks that it was weak and disordered when it reached the English position. A man-at-arms was not a headlong galloping cavalier, his attack could not be very rapid unless it was made in disorder; it was

29

shock-action, but shock of a ponderous column moving at a moderate rate.

The words put into the mouths of his fictional characters by Conan Doyle give a reasonable idea of the character and courage of the French soldiers, besides illustrating the difference between the peasant classes of the two countries.[1]

'The French are . . . very worthy men. We have had great good fortune in France, and it hath led to much bobnance and camp-fire talk, but I have ever noticed that those who know the most have the least to say about it. I have seen Frenchmen fight both in open field, in the intaking and the defending of towns or castlewicks, in escalados, camisades, night forays, bushments, sallies, outfalls and knightly spear-runnings. Their knights and squires, lad, are every whit as good as ours, and I could pick out a score of those who ride behind Du Guesclin who could hold the lists with sharpened lances against the best men in the army of England. On the other hand, their common folk are so crushed down with gabelle, and poll-tax, and every manner of cursed tallage, that the spirit has passed right out of them. It is a fool's plan to teach a man to be a cur in peace, and think that he will be a lion in war. If the nobles had not conquered the poor folk it is like enough that we should not have conquered the nobles. The men of the law are strong in France as well as the men of war. By my hilt! I hold that a man has more to fear there from the ink-pot of the one than from the iron of the other. There is ever some cursed sheepskin in their strongboxes to prove that the rich man should be richer and the poor man poorer. It would scarce pass in England but they are quiet folk over the water.'

The English infantry consisted of archers and foot spearmen; the latter were mostly from Wales. Although the longbow originated in that country, it soon crossed the border and first Cheshire men and then archers of other counties were armed with it; all the archers in Edward III's army were Englishmen. Edward III created a mounted archer corps in 1334, but foot archers were almost indistinguishable from mounted archers once the battle began. Both were similarly armed with a longbow, sword and dagger, both wore breastplates or padded hauberks and a steel cap; spearmen were similarly attired except that they

1. A. Conan Doyle, *The White Company*, p. 79. During the course of a conversation between John of Hordle, Alleyne Edricson and Aylward, the veteran bowman, when they discussed the respective merits of the Scots and the French as foemen of the English.

seldom wore breastplates. The archers could discharge the long-bow six times a minute at an effective range of 250 yards with an extreme range of 350 yards. French archers were armed with the crossbow, more powerful than the longbow but four arrows could be fired in the time it took to discharge one bolt. Usually used by Genoese mercenaries, it was more inaccurate and had a shorter range.

Little was heard of artillery in field operations, only surprise reaction being claimed for the cannon that Edward carefully nursed all the way to Crécy. But in siege operations the power of the cannon was steadily increasing, so that in the last years of the war it had a predominating effect in securing the surrender of defended towns and castles.

Edward's army had regular rates of pay; there is a record of the Prince of Wales's retinue:

7 bannerets at 4s. a day (a banneret was a knight entitled to carry a banner – each banneret was expected to find an archer for each man-at-arms he provided).

136 knights at 2s. a day.

143 esquires (rank-and-file men-at-arms) at 1s. a day.

900 mounted archers at 6d. a day.

Foot archers seem to have got sums ranging from 2d. to 4d. per day.

4

Their Way of Fighting

The age of the knight in armour will always possess a colour and glory because of its code of honour hallowed and revered by the upper classes in their attempts to render themselves worthy of their exceptional privileges. But much of the outward display and the class-conscious conventions on which such chivalry had always rested were swept away by the exigencies of serious warfare when the Hundred Years War brought national conflict between France and England. With such vast disparities of population – France had over ten million and England only three to four million[1] – the English leaders had to make the best use of the material at their disposal and were highly satisfied if their methods enabled them to beat the enemy. These commanders who made such good use of archery as a national tactic had no real conception of the fact that in terminating the ascendancy in war of the mailed horseman they were putting an end to the feudal regime and all that it entailed. Regarding themselves as the very flower of chivalry, Edward I, Edward III and the Black Prince might have paused in their efforts had they realised that their successful tactics meant the end of so-called chivalrous warfare. It could be that the needs of the moment prevented them having such thoughts, just as the fullest implications of Hiroshima were not realised in 1945.

Before archery became of supreme importance in warfare there existed a lengthy and tactically stagnant epoch when the mail-clad feudal horseman reigned supreme. Because the feudal organisation of society made every man of gentle blood a fighting-man, but not necessarily a soldier, a feudal army presented an unbelievable collection of unsoldierlike qualities. Although arrogance, stupidity and great courage coloured the activities of these armies, their inability to replace skill and experience made tactics and strategy impossible. The knight had no conception that discipline and tactical skill were as important as courage; it was always possible that at some inopportune and critical moment a battle might be precipitated or a carefully laid plan ruined by the incredibly foolish bravery of some petty knight with lust for only personal glory. Social status rather than professional experience led to command, so that the noble with the largest following was always superior to the skilled veteran with only a few lances to lead.

When a number of tenants-in-chief, all blindly jealous of each other, had been collected together with great difficulty they formed an unwieldy, unmanoeuvrable host ready to melt away from the standard the moment their short period of war-service was over. They recognised no superior but the King, and, unless he were a leader of uncommon skill, he was often powerless to control them, so that the radical vice of insubordination continued

1. The Black Death, a plague which struck Britain in 1349, swept away more than half of the three or four millions who then formed the population of England. So fierce were its assaults that the whole organisation of labour was thrown out of gear and for a time even cultivation ceased. Nearly 60,000 people perished in Norwich, whilst in Bristol the living were hardly able to bury the dead. The respective numerical strengths of the French and English armies must be viewed in the light of this situation.

unchecked. Their very formation encouraged this in many ways; confined to a single pattern, they were formed into three great masses or battles and then launched at the enemy; there could really be no other way because the troops were neither disciplined nor accustomed to act together so that combined movements of small bodies were impossible.

Keeping a reserve in hand was a refinement practised by very few commanders, partly because it would have been very difficult to persuade a feudal chief to stay out of the front line of battle so that he incurred the risk of missing some of the hard fighting. Regarded as a model of military efficiency if he could sit his charger steadily and skilfully handle a sword and lance, nothing could restrain him when the enemy came in sight. His shield would be shifted into position, the lance dropped into rest, the spur plunged into the charger and the mail-clad line would ponderously roll forward. Thundering on as they gained speed, they had little regard for anything that might lie before them; as often as not the formation dashed themselves against a stone wall or tumbled into a ditch; painfully floundered in a bog or surged futilely around a wall or palisade. If the enemy were similar to themselves the two forces would meet with a fearful shock, men and horses tumbling in all directions, and then a chaotic mêlée would follow, sometimes lasting for hours. This meant that most engagements were nothing more than a huge, sprawling scuffle and scramble of men and horses over a patch of bare land or a hillside. Sometimes, as if by general agreement, both parties would laboriously wheel to the rear, halt for a while as their horses regained breath, and then rush at each other again until one side was worsted and fled from the field. The most elementary military tactics, such as preselecting a battle position, or using a reserve to take the enemy in rear or flank were considered examples of exceptional military skill. The commendation of the age boiled down to striking individual feat of arms rather than any efforts at real leadership.

Great battles did not take place very often, simply because opposing armies often completely lost each other because they neglected to keep in touch by vedettes or outposts and patrols. It was usually the existence of some topographical objective, such as a road, ford or bridge, which precipitated a conflict; with maps non-existent and geographical knowledge both scanty and inaccurate, it was easy for armies to stray away and lose sight of each other. A recognised manner in which this last contingency was prevented lay in the opposing generals solemnly sending and accepting challenges to meet in battle at a given place and on a definite date.

There was little for the infantry to do, no important part for them to play; they accompanied the armies for no better purpose than to perform the menial camp duties and assist in the numerous sieges of the period. Now and then, as a sort of overture, they were used to demonstrate ineffectually at the opening of a battle, but if they presumed to prolong these demonstrations, their lords, affronted by such presumption, would end the skirmishing by riding into and over their luckless followers. The half-armed peasants and burghers who had unwillingly joined the levy because it was the duty of every able-bodied man to do so were incapable of combining to withstand a cavalry charge; lacking adequate weapons and without discipline, they were ridden down and crushed.

The only infantry who commanded any respect were those bodies who were armed with more or less uniform equipment and weapons; the chief cause of the military unworthiness of infantry generally can be said to have been due primarily to the miscellaneous nature of their armament. The Scottish lowlanders, with their long spears, and the Saracen auxiliaries, plying their crossbows, stood out as troops capable of putting up good performances on foot and without all the benefits of high birth. The few infantry successes which occurred towards the end of the feudal period were exceptional and served to foreshadow the new era of co-ordinated dismounted warfare.

When a feudal host came up against a force or a commander capable of exercising even the most simple and rudimentary tactics on the field of battle they invariably took a hiding. With each commander making his own speed into the attack, followed by his supporters, the feudal force arrived at the scene of battle in small scattered groups. This meant that the battle was made up of a number of detached and unco-ordinated cavalry combats and a systematic enemy could defeat each of these groups in detail so that the sum total of the small routs added up to a great defeat. In this way a skirmish, a street fight or the bogging-down of a group of heavily armed horsemen could overthrow an entire force.

With such an unscientific method of warfare, resembling nothing more than a huge tilting-match, it only needed one side to bring into the field a factor that would prevent their opponents from approaching near enough to break a lance for the whole concept of then-known warfare to break down. By introducing auxiliaries like the English archer against a military caste too hidebound and blind to alter its losing methods throughout almost the whole of a hundred-year period, the English commanders could hardly fail to bring to earth the flower of French chivalry. French chivalry was to receive an early and striking lesson when the peasant-archer faced the high-born knight at Crécy in 1346. It was a lesson that was to be unheeded, in spite of finding himself unable to approach the position from which the deadly arrow reached him, the knight still clung to the tradition which gave the most honourable name in war to the mounted man. Thus were cavalry, whose day had really passed, perpetuated for another century; a system so intimately bound up with mediaeval life and customs would take more than a single disaster, or the dozen others to follow, before being irretrievably smashed.

5

The English Archer

'We'll all drink together
To the grey goose feather,
And the land where the grey goose flew.
What of the men?
The men were bred in England,
The Bowmen, the yeomen,
The lads of dale and fell.
Here's to you and to you
To the hearts that are true,
And the land where the true hearts dwell.'
Marching Song of the White Company
CONAN DOYLE

The whole history of English warfare from the middle of the twelfth century to the end of the fifteenth century proves that the flower of her infantry was the archers. The bow was put in the hand of every English boy at the age of seven and it did not cease to furnish him with sport and occupation until the years had deprived his arm of strength and his eye of skill. From the

Conquest down to the general introduction of the musket, the use and practice of the longbow were enforced by some form or other of English legislature. The English archer was not only a singular man of war, he also possessed a singular status unlike anything else in Continental Europe; it was a status that made him the fighting man he was, capable of standing to the death if ordered or making a sudden flank attack on his own initiative when the situation demanded. He was not a peasant bound to someone superior in birth and position, he was a freeman, a yeoman who gave his valuable fighting services in return for a contract setting out his rate of pay and term of service.

History and fiction give many descriptions of the archer; most of them picture him as a Robin Hood-like man dressed in Lincoln green and wearing a hat of a well-known shape, with a fancy feather rising from its side. In the pages of his *Canterbury Tales* Geoffrey Chaucer shows us his archer:

> 'And he was clad in cote and hood of grene;
> A sheefe or pecock-arrowes brighte and keene
> Under his belt he bar ful thriftily;
> (Wel coude he dresse his taken yemanly;
> His arrowes drouped nought with fetheres lowe,)
> And in his hand he bar a mighty bowe;
> A not-heed haddle he, with a broun visage.
> Of wodecraft wel coude he al the usage.
> Under his arm he bar a gay bracer,
> And by his syde a swerd and a bokeler,
> And on that other syde a gay daggere,
> Harneised wel, and sharp as point of spere;
> A Cristofre on his brest of silver shene.
> A horn he bar, the baudrick was of grene.'

Less colourful, but of a more warlike nature, is the description of the English archer given by one Ralphe Smithe:

'Captains and officers should be skilful of that most noble weapon, and to see that their soldiers according to their draught and strength, have good bows, well nocked, well strynged, everie strynge whippe in their nock, and in the middles rubbed with wax; baser and shooting-glove; some spare strynges as aforesaid. Everie man one shefe of arrows with a case of leather, defensible against the rayne; and in the same foure-and-twenty arrows, whereof eight of them should be lighter than the residue to gall or astonye the enemy with the hail-shot of light arrows.

Let everie man have a brigandine, or little cote of plate; a skull (cap), or hufkin; a maul of lead, five feet in length; and a pike, and the same hanging by his side, with a hook and dagger. Being thus furnished, teach them by their masters to march, shoote and retyre, keeping their faces to the enemy. Some time put them in great nowmbers, as to battell appertayneth, and thus use them oftentymes till they be perfecte; for those men in battell or skirmish cannot be spared.'

It seems reasonable to assume, because of the physical training that their practice entailed, that the archers were strong, muscular men; tall, sinewy, brown, clear-eyed and hard-visaged – middle-sized or tall men of big and robust build, with arching chests and extraordinary breadth of shoulder. The older soldiers were grizzled and lean, with fierce puckered features and shaggy bristling brows, skin tanned and dried by the weather. The younger men had fresh, English faces, with beards combed out and hair curling from under their close, steel hufkins. Their profession was proclaimed by the yew or hazel stave slung over their shoulder, plain and serviceable with the older men but gaudily painted and carved at either end when belonging to younger archers. Steel caps, mail brigandines, white surcoats with the red Lion of St George, and sword or battleaxe swinging from their belts completed the equipment. In some cases the murderous maul or five-foot mallet was hung across the bow-stave, being fastened to their leathern shoulder-belt by a hook in the centre of the handle. When they went to war, spare bow-staves were taken, plus three spare cords allowed for each bow and a great store of arrow-heads.

According to his strength and height, so the archer equipped himself. The tall and muscular man of six feet and upwards found that a powerful bow of seven feet was best suited to his purpose and his arrows were a cloth-yard, besides the head. His smaller comrade would use a six-foot bow and shorter arrows, reducing them to the correct length if they were too long for him, although it appears to have been quite usual for archers to fix loose arrow-heads to their own shafts. It is said that at Agincourt the army of Henry V consisted of such tremendous archers that most of them drew a yard. Tall men, with strength and length of arm, could draw the clothyard shaft, others adapted themselves to the arrow lengths they could handle. Sir Samuel Rush Meyrick, author of an old history of arms and armour, wrote:

'With respect to the size of the bow, the string ought to be the height of the man, and the arrow half the length of the string. Now, as from that, to the top of the middle finger, is equal to half his whole height, it must be equal also to the length of his arrow; and the left hand, therefore, being clenched round the bow, will leave just room for the arrow-head beyond it. From this it will appear that a man six feet high must shoot with a clothyard arrow and vice versa.'

English archers carried into the field a sheaf of twenty-four barbed arrows, buckled within their girdles. A portion of them, about six or eight, were longer, lighter and winged with narrower feathers than the rest. With these flight arrows, as they were called, they could hit a mark at a greater distance than with the remaining heavy sheaf arrows. The advantages occasionally derived from this superiority of range, when directed by a skilful leader, have led to very important results such as that at Towton. Unfledged arrows cannot fly far and are greatly affected by the wind. Ascham, the 'Izaak Walton of archery', says: 'Neither wood, horn, metal, parchment, paper nor cloth but only a feather is fit for a shaft.' There must have been a great consumption of goose feathers; and army needed at least 20,000 sheaves of arrows, requiring a million and a half goose feathers. Peacock feathers were used as well as those of the grey goose:

> 'With everie arrowe an ell long,
> With peacocke well y dyght.'

The archer had to find a style which was reasonably natural and which consequently came fairly automatically; if the English archers shot by instinct then it was in the knowledge of how much force to use that this instinct came in. But it was not really an innate skill, it was one nurtured and fostered by years of practice, beginning at about seven to nine years of age. Then the lad would hold out a round stick in his left hand, arm stiff and straight from the shoulder; as silent and still as a small statue, the lad would hold out the stick until his arm was as heavy as lead – in this way the left arm was trained to have a steady grasp of the bow. When he became older and could bend a war-bow so as to be able to bring down a squirrel at a hundred paces, then a boy was ready to be considered suitable to become an archer in the King's army. Even then it was still necessary to practise – in fact, it was compulsory.

During their off-duty periods the young archers would throw aside their coats of mail or leather hauberks, set down their steel skull-caps, and turn back their jerkins to give free play to their brawny chests and arms. Standing in line, they would each loose a shaft in turn, while the older, experienced bowmen lounged up and down the line with critical eyes and words of rough praise or curt censure for each marksman. Now and then they could cry out advice:

'Loose it easy, steady and yet sharp!'

'Don't wink with one eye and look with the other! Nay, lad! You don't need to hop and dance after you shoot – that won't speed it on its way! Stand firm and straight, as God made you. Move not the bow-arm and steady with the drawing hand.'

The scarred and grizzled veterans knew that it was one thing to shoot at a target-shield, but another thing when there was a man behind that shield, riding at you with a wave of sword or lance, and eyes glinting from behind a closed visor – then it became a less easy mark!

Representations of the old longbowmen in the ancient illuminated manuscripts of the thirteenth to the fifteenth centuries identify the old stance and practice with the modern. A pen-and-ink drawing by John de Rous, a bowman as well as a contemporary biographer of the Earl of Warwick, shows the necessary slight inclination of the head and neck – this 'laying of the body into the bow' – the drawing with two and with three fingers, are correctly delineated. This drawing is among the MSS. at the British Museum. A sixteenth-century verse says:

'Who thought it then a manlie sight and trim
To see a youth of clean, compacted limb,
Who with a comely grace, in his left hand,
Holding his bow, did take his steadfast stand,
Setting his left foot somewhat forth before,
His arrow with his right hand nocking sure,
Not stooping, nor yet standing straight upright,
Then, with his left hand little 'bove his sight,
Stretching his arm out, with an easy strength,
To draw an arrow of a yard in length.'

The English longbowmen might well have appeared to aim instinctively because it was quicker, but they really took careful aim, using their judgment to determine the height of their aim. Over the course of hundreds of years it has been proven that the best manner of using a bow is to use the same force for every shot regardless of whether the target is close or far away. This is exactly what the English archer did – he used the full power of his bow every time, never instinctively using more or less of it in order to reach his mark. The bow being held perpendicularly to the ground, their stance was sideways on to their target; in this way the best use could be made of the muscles needed for drawing a war-bow into such a position that the arrow in the bow lay under the eye. This stance also meant that they could stand closer together, thus better concentrating their volleys, which were made even more effective by the rear ranks being able to fire over the heads of the men in front of them.

The best archers looked comfortable and free from awkwardness – a good stance was always graceful and never ugly – competent archery lends itself admirably to the statuesque position. With the bow held out by one arm pointing towards the mark or target, the head was turned in the same direction only as far as was comfortable. The other hand, drawing the string back with the arrow 'nocked' on to it, was brought to such a position under or alongside the chin that the tail of the arrow was at a point under the aiming eye. To make sure that the arrow was brought back to the same point under the eye every time, the string would touch one point on the face – on the chin, the lips or the nose. The chin, either right in the middle or at some spot on the side, was the commonest; the lips were the most sensitive and made it possible to detect more easily any slight variation to one side of the proper place. The drawing-hand was, at the same time, brought back firmly to its 'anchor-point' (a definite 'anchor-point' was of the utmost importance as it very largely influenced the accuracy of the aim for elevation). If the knuckle at the base of the first finger came up against the angle of the jaw, an almost foolproof anchor-point was obtained.

After reaching the full-draw position there was a brief pause before the arrow was sent on its deadly way; during which the aim was finally taken. Now was the time when practice, instinct, innate ability, and all the other factors that made one archer better than another, came into play. Instinctively, the bowman checked all the other vital points in his stance – his bodily balance, the pressure of the fingers of both hands, the position of the elbows, the anchor-point, the angle of the bow, but especially the length of the draw.

The more expert the archer, the shorter the period of holding; and it was always the same length of time – every fraction of a second over his normal holding period, with the bow held at full draw, took something away from the cast of the bow and caused the arrow to fall short. During the whole act of shooting, from the beginning of the draw until after the arrow was loosed, the archer held his breath, with lungs just normally filled. The action of shooting was not hurried, the same time was taken with each arrow; the English archer acquired a regular rhythm. He would rather come down and start again if he were not satisfied – better that than to take a chance with what he knew to be a bad arrow.

When the whole body was under tension at full-draw, concentration reached its peak as the slight final movement of the bow-arm was made to complete the aim. Rather than force their arms to move fractionally in their sockets, some archers would shift their body weight a trifle on to the rear foot. All knew that it was best to bring the bow-hand up to the required elevation just before or at the moment the draw was completed; in this way only a very minute adjustment was needed after the shaft-hand had been finally anchored. Every archer developed some little characteristic action or movement that distinguished him from his fellows; he sought to settle down into a style which suited him best, because it was comfortable and automatic, bringing maximum success.

When Henry V addressed his archers before Agincourt he endeavoured to fire them by dwelling on the cruelties in store for them should they fall into the hands of the French, who, he said, had sworn to amputate their first three fingers so that they would never more slay man or horse. Many an English archer, captured by French or Scots, could ruefully hold up two hands to show that the thumbs and first two fingers had been torn away from each. His comrades set a vengeful value on them – twenty enemy lives for the thumbs and half a score for the fingers. From this, the importance of the archer's fingers is emphasised – every archer sought for a 'sharp loose'; acquired by an apparent although not actual, feeling of increasing the pull of the fingers on the string until it suddenly and instantaneously slipped off the fingers without any sign of creeping, or any feel that the fingers had relaxed. Most of the feel of drawing should be put into the first finger; the string starting quite close up to the first joint on that finger and sloping away across the middle of the first joint of the second finger, finishing up almost at the tip of the third finger, which will then be prevented from doing too much. A very 'sharp loose' could be got in this way, as the first finger, the lazy one, was under better control.

The first finger was the strongest but the laziest; the second was also strong and not noticeably temperamental, it would generally follow the first finger; the third finger was the weakest, but it was also the most willing and could be hurt if it did more than its proper share of drawing.

The older archers endeavoured to instil into the beginners the need to lay the body to the bow, to draw from the thigh and hip as much as from the arm. To learn to shoot with a dropping shaft was essential; and arrow will go a certain distance up into the air before it falls towards its mark – when an arrow has its point directly on the target to be hit there is only one distance at which the arrow will fall on to the mark itself. This is 'point-blank' range and for an average man drawing a bow of, say, forty-two-pound draw-weight (under half that of the old English archer) that distance will be somewhere between 80 and 100 yards. An adjustment had to be made in the aim for elevation when shooting at a distance longer or shorter than point-blank range, bearing in mind that the bow was always drawn to the same extent so that the same power was used each time. This was done by selecting a point at which to aim either, for shorter distances, on the ground short of the target, or, for longer distances, in a tree or some other tall object above and behind the target. In the latter case, this often meant that the mark was obscured by the bow-hand, but the line of the arrow was constantly under observation.

An archer was often called upon to shoot straight and fast; but often he had to deal with an enemy hiding behind a wall or an arbalestier with his mantlet (a wooden shield) raised – the only way in which such protected men could be hit was to fire in such a manner that the shaft fell upon them straight from the clouds. Even as early as Richard I's siege of Messina, the archers drove the Sicilians from the walls in this manner – 'for no man could look out of doors but he would have an arrow in his eye before he could shut it.'

It is evident from the fact that they wore no defensive armour that the archers were designed to be light infantry, swift and mobile, skilful and deadly with their weapons. The name of Edward I must ever be memorable in history for the encouragement he gave to the longbow. But we seek in vain for the man who founded the tradition that the English, whatever their weapon, should always be good shots – the English archer was reputed to be able to draw and discharge his bow twelve times in a single minute, at a range of 250 yards, and if he once missed his man in these twelve shots he was but lightly esteemed.

Here it is difficult to separate fact from fiction; the old

chroniclers ventured away from accuracy when describing the feats of the English archer, that is highly possible – but, to counter it, there are many modern archers who can emulate and best the reputed feats of Robin Hood and his men! For a weary and sick army of less than 6,000 men to defeat over 25,000 French at Agincourt must indicate that the archers could notch with a shaft every crevice and joint of a man-at-arms' harness, from the clasp of his bascinet to the hinge of his greave. With that in mind, can we calmly discount the story of the Genoan crossbowman who raised his arm over his mantlet and shook his fist at the English, a hundred paces from him? Twenty of the English bowmen immediately loosed shafts at him, and when the man was afterwards slain, it was found that he had taken eighteen shafts through his forearm. Or, the account of two English archers firing at the hempen anchor-cord of the captured English cog *Christopher* held in Calais harbour – at 200 paces the archers in four shots had cut every strand of the cord so that the boat went on to the rocks!

Well authenticated fiction about the period, with copious use of the chronicles of such as Froissart, can tell much about the performances of these semi-legendary characters who so moulded mediaeval English history. One can read in *The White Company* by A. Conan Doyle of a contest between a crossbowman of Brabant and an English archer who says:

'To my mind, the longbow is a better weapon than the arbalest; I will venture a rover with you, or try the long butts or hoyles.' The veteran selects a Scotch bow, recognisable because the upper nock is without and the lower within – 'A good piece of yew, well nocked, well strung, well waxed and very joyful to the feel.' He is very careful about the arrows that he uses –'. . . I love an ash arrow pierced with cornel-wood for a roving shaft . . . it has been my mind to choose a saddle-backed feather for a dead shaft and a swine-backed for a smooth flier . . .'

The crossbowman, impatient at such slow and methodical actions, drew his moulinet from his girdle and, fixing it to the windlass, draws back the powerful double cord until it clicked into the catch. Then from his quiver he drew a short thick quarrel, which he placed with the utmost care upon the groove. Before he could fire at the nominated mark, a large grey stork flapped heavily into view with a peregrine falcon poised over its head, awaiting its opportunity of darting down on its clumsy victim. When the pair were a hundred paces from them the crossbowman raised his weapon to the sky and there came the short, deep twang of his powerful string. His bolt struck the stork just where its wing meets the body, and the bird whirled aloft in a last convulsive flutter before falling wounded and flapping to the earth. At the instant that the bolt struck its mark, the old archer, hitherto standing listless with arrow on string, bent his bow and sped a shaft through the body of the falcon. Whipping another arrow from his girdle, he sent it skimming a few feet from the earth to strike and transfix the stork for a second time before it could touch the ground.

In this way the archer proved that the longbow could do what the crossbow could not, for even the most expert arbalestier could not speed another shaft skywards before the bird had reached the round, as did the archer.

In the nature of trick-shooting probably of little use in actual warfare is the shooting of an arrow so that it covers vast distances – a mile in three flights is recorded, as is a length of 630 paces. To do this the archer would use a bow of exceptional size and strength; sitting down upon the ground he would place his two feet at either end of the stave. With an arrow fitted, he then pulled the string towards him with both hands until the head of the shaft was level with the wood. The great bow would creak and groan and the cord vibrate with the tension; the archer raised his two feet, with the bow-stave on their soles, and his cord twanged with a deep rich hum that could be heard for a considerable distance as the arrow sped on its way.

During the contest between the archer and crossbowman that has already been mentioned, both fire at a shield made of inch-thick elm with a bull's hide over it. The bolt from the crossbow is driven deeply into the wood; the archer carefully greases his shaft and sends it towards the shield. On inspection, the shield has a round clear hole in the wood at the back of it, showing that the arrow has passed through it.

English archers tried to avoid fighting with the sun in their front, considering the dazzling splendour of a summer's day to be very unfavourable to shooting. At Crécy, when the sudden gleam of sunshine after the rain burst forth behind the English, its beams, besides dazzling the eyes of the enemy, flashed upon their polished shields and corselets with a lustre so brilliant that the archers discharged their first flight of arrows with more than usual certainty of aim. Wind and weather will likewise exercise a certain influence upon even the most superbly directed arrow; for shooting in boisterous weather, a comparatively heavy arrow does best.

In addition to being incomparable with his missile weapon, the English archer would frequently discard his bow and fight on foot with sword, axe or maul. When a knight was seated on a horse it was almost impossible to get any power into a swing with a sword, so that he had to stand up to deliver his blow. Standing in the stirrups, he left exposed the one unprotected part in his whole armoured body – his seat. This was the target of the nimble archers and they seldom missed with their keen swords as they dodged on light feet in and out of the horse and foot mêlée.

Well might Sir John Fortescue say:

'The might of the realme of England standyth upon archers.'

6

His Longbow

'What of the bow?
　The bow was made in England,
Of true wood, of yew wood,
　The wood of English bows;
For men who are free
　Love the old yew-tree
And the land where the yew-tree grows.'
Marching Song of the White Company
CONAN DOYLE

Apart from some rough unfinished staves in the Tower of London recovered, in 1841, from the wreck of the *Mary Rose* sunk in 1545, and the remains of an early bow dug up at Berkhamsted Castle, thought to have dated from the siege of 1217, and now in the British Museum – there are probably no surviving specimens of the tens of thousands of longbows made during the Middle Ages.

There is little reason for any of them to be preserved; it was a weapon of the common man, kept in the corner of lowly cottages and then only if fit for use. The war-bow was not a decoration to be hung on the walls of castles, manors and great houses, along with the swords, shields and lances of ancestral knights. The old bow had nothing sufficiently artistic about it for it to form an attractive ornament for the wall after its useful life was over. If used long enough, every good bow eventually broke or developed faults that made it useless for anything except firewood – no inferior weapon could be retained by the English archer because his very life depended upon its efficiency.

It cannot be claimed that the longbow contributed towards the foundation of the British Empire; but it may well have gone a long way towards discouraging other countries and powers from attempting to add England to their empires. It was, in fact, simply a primitive form of artillery, playing the same part then as now – softening up the enemy to allow the infantry to get to grips under the most advantageous conditions. There are numerous instances of archers being used in most intelligent fashion to cover the movement of other troops – a 'combined operation' at the landing of English men-at-arms at Cadzand, in 1346, enabled them to get comfortably ashore whilst the defenders were pinned down by hails of arrows from massed archers. In the autumn of 1342 Robert of Artois was besieging Vannes, then second city of Brittany; after spending the first few days in making preparations for the assault D'Artois delivered it early one morning. The archers put down what would now be called a 'standing barrage' on to the battlements – so fierce and accurate that, according to Froissart, the battlements were soon cleared and not an enemy dared show his head. Covered by this fire, the men-at-arms advanced to the assault; but the town actually fell at night when a feint attack drew defenders from the walls to the gates, thus permitting small parties of English to scale the walls and attack from within.

In the summer of 1344 the Earl of Derby was attacking the town of Bergerac in Gascony, using the fleet on the river Dordogne in a combined land-and-water attack on a portion of the wall close to the river. Vessels were filled with archers, who, as soon as a breach had been made in the wall, kept up such a heavy fire that the garrison did not dare venture into the open to repair it. Others engaged in a long duel with Genoese crossbowmen in the town to draw their fire from the breach. The ranges at which these operations took place are not known, but the longbow had an effective range of 200 – 240 yards; Shakespeare says 290 yards (*Henry IV*, Part 2, Act III, Scene ii). Edward VI's 'Journal' states that the King's archers could completely pierce a board one inch thick.

The skill and deadliness of the English archer were not a matter of chance; the law prescribed the bow-weights which were proper for youths of various ages, because the weapon was little use without special training. Bishop Latimer wrote: 'My father was diligent in teaching me to shoot with the bow; he taught me to draw, to lay my body to the bow, not to draw with the strength of the arm as other nations do, but with the strength of the body. I had my bows bought me according to my age and strength; as I increased in these my bows were made bigger and bigger.' With so much practice and legislature to ensure that it was carried out, it is small wonder that the yeomen of England could pull a war-bow of 100 lb. or more with ease and skill. Incidentally, the contract price of a bow in 1341 was – unpainted, 1s.; painted, 1s. 6d.; a sheaf of twenty-four arrows cost 1sh. 2d. and the archers received pay amounting to 3d. per day.

The war-bow was about six feet in length and usually pulled 100 lb.; the strength of the bow was calculated by the power whereby it restores itself to its natural position, according to the distance from which it is removed; here the physical strength of the archer is the deciding factor in the effective range. It was usually self-nocking; that is, the nocks for the string at top and bottom were integral parts of the bow itself. Fancier bows had horn or ivory nocks fastened to the ends of the bow limbs. In cross-section the longbow looked like a letter 'D' lying on its back; the belly of the bow faced the shooter, formed the round of the 'D', whilst the back, facing the target, was flat. Although from a standpoint of design the longbow was wasteful of both wood and energy, the English used it without that fact being known, nor does it appear to have detracted from its efficacy.

Into the making of a good English longbow went a great deal of fine craftsmanship – it had to be tapered correctly, with much patience and experience, from the middle towards each end so that it was brought to an even curve at full draw. All knots and irregularities in the grain had to be carefully watched and 'raised' or skilfully followed to eliminate weak spots. Except in the very rare case of a perfect stave, the finished article was a knobbly length of wood lacking in beauty. There were no cunningly carved horn nocks on the ends, merely simple grooves cut into the wood itself to take the loops of the bowstring; there was no velvet or leather padded grip at the centre; no mother-of-pearl arrow-plate let into the side of the stave where the shaft rested against it, so that the arrow was prevented from wearing a groove as it passed.

The crossbow was an intricate and complicated mechanism with much metal work about it – but the longbow was a plain, rather ugly stick. It was almost as crude in appearance as a wooden club that could be cut from any tree or hedgerow, in spite of the careful workmanship that went into it. Infinitely greater artistry went into the fashioning of arrow-heads; there are plenty of specimens to be seen in museums but few complete shafts remain.

The English archer was accustomed to no other sort of bow than the styled 'self' or formed of a single piece. When summoned on domestic military service, the archers, except those living on Crown lands, came armed into the field; if they were engaged on foreign expeditions, the necessary equipment was provided at public cost. The bows themselves were of many woods. The chronicles seem wrong in invariably listing bows as being made of English yew; although the best wood was undoubtedly yew, it came from trees sought in all the mountainous parts of Spain, Portugal, Italy and Germany. At one time Spain had supplied England with many of the rough bowstaves of yew – but Spain herself had suffered raids by English bowmen under the Black Prince, which so affronted Spanish pride that the legends say that all yew trees were cut down after the invasion and allowed to grow no more for fear the English would come again, plying bows of Spanish yew! A comparatively small number of bows were made of English yew because little of it grew in England, and that mostly in churchyards or other enclosed places where cattle could not reach its poisonous leaves. English yew was too quick-grown and coarse-grained to make a really good bow; it was so knotty and defective that no part could be relied upon, except that portion of the heart protected by the exterior stratum of sapwood. Other woods were also used, probably for compulsory practice purposes, among them wych-elm, ash and hazel, but the slow-grown mountain yew is, to this day, the supreme wood for the longbow of traditional English pattern.

In making a yew self-bow the entire butt of a clean tree, inside as well as outside, can be used, provided that the staves are not sawn but cleft from the plank. One old authority claims that the best is that nearest the outside of the log, consisting of practically all the light-coloured sapwood immediately under the bark and only as much of the darker heartwood as may be needed. This combination of sapwood and heartwood in yew provides the two essential properties – the sapwood is resistant to stretch and is therefore suitable for the back (the convex side when the bow is bent); and the heartwood resists compression and is, for that

48

reason, perfect for the belly of the bow. In fact, the heartwood will not stretch at all if bent the 'wrong' way, but bursts immediately. Because of this, a broken string usually meant a broken bow in the case of a yew bow, because the bow flew back unchecked by the string to a point beyond its natural position of rest.

Ascham, the patron of the longbow, wrote: 'The best colour of a bow is when the back and belly in working are much alike; for oft-times in wearing, it proves like virgin wax or gold.' In other words, it became silky, smooth and took a fine polish.

Since the old war-bows were made in one piece from end to end, there might well be considerable changes in the properties of the wood in such a six-foot length – the thickness of the sapwood and direction of the grain might vary, together with the incidence of knots and pins. This meant that very great skill had to be exercised in shaping the limbs to obtain equal bending in both. It seems likely that there was tremendous difficulty in finding long staves fit for first-class bows in the numbers required; the obvious inequalities in these old bows giving them a very short life of useful work and little chance of survival to the present day. As England alone was quite unable to meet the supply of bow-staves demanded, it was necessary to import them; this often meant that they came in at prices which put them out of reach of the ordinary common man. To combat this, the government of the day hit upon a clever scheme or expedient to render them as inexpensive as possible.

Since all timber possesses a harder texture and a finer grain when grown in a warm climate than when reared in one less gentle, the traders and merchants of Lombardy were compelled to deliver a certain quantity of foreign yew with every cask of Greek and Italian wine admitted into the London custom-house. Edward IV, with whom this law originated, fixed the number of bow-staves at four, but Richard III, his successor, increased them to ten for each butt. The merchants would have yew trees, already lopped and trimmed, conveyed to the ports, where they selected enough, at a rough guess, to equal the wine on board and made them useful as dunnage among the casks. Bow-staves were also imported for cash; under Richard III a law was passed which complained of the mendacity of the Lombard traders, who had caused inflation in the price. Formerly 100 staves had brought £2, but due to the traders' machinations the price had risen to £8. It was to counter price increases originally that the wood and wine law was passed.

The old authority, Ashcam, speaking of the quality of bows,

said: 'A good bow is known by the proof. If you come to a shop and see one that is small, long, heavy and strong, lying straight and not winding or marred with knots, buy that bow on my warrant. The short-grained bow is for the most part brittle. Every bow is made of the bough or plant of a tree. The former is commonly very knotty, small, weak and will soon follow the string. The latter proveth many times well, if it be of a good clean growth; and, if the pith is good, it will ply and bend before it breaks. Let the staves be good and even chosen, and afterwards wrought as the grain of the wood leadeth a man, or else the bow must break, and that soon, in shivers. This must be considered in the rough wood. You must not stick for a groat or two more than another man would give for a good bow; for such a one twice paid for is better than an ill one once broken. Thus a shooter must begin, not at the making of his bow like a bowyer, but at the buying of his bow like an archer. Before he trust his bow, let him take it into the fields and shoot with dead, heavy shafts. Look where it cometh most, and provide for that place, lest it pinch and so frete. Thus when you have shot him, and perceive good wood in him, you must take him to a good workman, which shall cut him shorter and dress him fitter, make him come round compass everwhere.'

Bowstrings of the era were made of a good grade of flax or linen and, when strung, were impregnated with beeswax so as to repel rain and dew. The bowman would watch his string carefully and if it showed signs of fraying, especially at the loops, he scrapped it before it broke. With a good yew bow, a broken string often meant a broken bow. Spare strings were always carefully broken in at practice – a new string never shot at first in the same way as the old one; archers were required to carry two spare bowstrings.

Most archers carried twenty-four arrows at their side, in their belt or girdle – in battle they were taken from the girdle and placed head-first in the ground immediately in front of the archer's position, within easy reach of his hand. The arrows were of varying lengths but generally they were described as 'clothyard shafts'; they were fitted with a barb and point of iron, fledged with feathers of goose or peacock. An arrow-head found, many years after the battle, on the field of Agincourt showed that it was made specially to pierce armour; the ferrule by which the head was originally attached to the wood was still perfect, but its diameter proved that the shaft could not have measured more than twenty-eight, or, at the most, thirty, inches.

In an ancient Act of Parliament it is stated: '*Tres pedes faciunt ulnam*' – (Three feet make an ell) – this establishes an identity with the clothier's yard at the most glorious period in the history of ancient archery. On no other supposition can the indiscriminate use of 'yard' and 'ell' by historians when talking of arrows be justified. As a Flemish ell measured twenty-seven inches, and a modern English ell forty-five inches, it would seem that an arrow might well have been less than an actual yard in length.

The arrow-heads used in this great period were tipped with little iron 'piles' no broader than the shafts upon which they were set. They were small heads with a bodkin-point, like a small cold-chisel, square or diamond in section, about two inches long and about half an inch square at the widest point, tapering to a sharp point; it was a solid chunk of iron with four barbs fitted to the shaft by a short socket. Against this tiny head and the enormous 'muzzle-velocity' behind it, chain-mail was no protection and it could even burst through plate-armour when a square hit was obtained. But plate-armour was more likely than not to deflect the shaft, hence the reason for its rapid development after Crécy had impressed upon an astounded Europe that the English bowman was a new power with which to reckon.

The effectiveness of these arrows is accentuated when one considers the much lighter modern hunting arrow, broad-headed and shot from a bow of perhaps 65 lb. weight; such an arrow is quite capable of cutting its way right through a deer and will easily penetrate a thousand sheets of paper as used in telephone directories. When fitted with a blunt, flat-ended cylindrical steel head, having the diameter of the shaft of the arrow, it readily penetrates an inch of pine board.

PART TWO

THE TACTICS ARE FORGED

7

Falkirk sets the Pattern – 1298

Edward I, being the man he was, wholeheartedly encouraged the use of the longbow, having seen for himself how effective it could be when properly handled; its potentialities had been brought to his notice by some of the extremely able soldiers who had fought for both sides during the civil wars in the 1260's. He used the traditional enmity of the Scots for the English to provide arrow fodder for the longbow in the experimenting hands of the English archers. These early Anglo-Scots battles seem to have made no impression upon those responsible for military affairs in France. When the now well-tried techniques were used in the early battles of the Hundred Years War they seem to have taken the French completely by surprise.

Following their victory over the English at Stirling Bridge on 13th September 1297 the triumphant Scots so ravaged the English border counties that the enraged Edward was forced to conclude a hasty treaty with the King of France and rush home. He reached England in mid-March 1298; instantly he summoned the barons and their captains to meet him at York on the Feast of Pentecost. The army assembled. In June Edward led his forces into Scotland by the eastern borders with the idea of marching into the western counties and crushing the rebellion of the Scots, as he termed the affair.

The army he reviewed at Roxburgh consisted of English, Welsh and Irish infantry, with a powerful body of mailed, mounted and well-disciplined cavalry, the veterans of his French wars; in addition he had with him a mounted corps of Gascons. They probably numbered 10,000 foot and about 2,500 horses. To oppose them William Wallace, the Scots leader, collected a force largely composed of armed peasantry organised as spearmen and armed with pikes some eleven feet in length. He also had a group of archers from the Ettrick Forest and a force of about 500 cavalry under John Comyn, son of the Lord of Badenoch. They were considerably less in number than the English army, but they had great confidence in their leader, who had positioned them in a very strong site to await battle.

That the Scots were formidable opponents is borne out by the very discerning opinion of the archer in Conan Doyle's book, *The White Company*:

' "I have heard that the Scots are good men of war," said Hordle John.

' "For axemen and for spearmen I have not seen their match," the archer answered. "They can travel, too, with bag of meal and grid-iron slung to their sword-belt, so that it is ill to follow them. There are scant crops and few beeves in the borderland, where a man must reap his grain with sickle in one fist and brown bill in the other. On the other hand, they are the sorriest archers that I have ever seen, and cannot so much as aim with the arbalest, to say nought of the longbow. Again, they are mostly poor folk, even the nobles among them, so that there are few who can buy as good a brigandine of chain mail as that which I am wearing, and it is ill for them to stand up against our own knights, who carry the price of five Scotch farms upon their chests and shoulders. Man for man, with equal weapons, they are as worthy and valiant men as could be found in the whole of Christendom." '

Their position was fronted by Darnrig Moss, a marsh through which no cavalry could pass; the flanks had been skilfully protected by field-works of wood palisades driven deep into the earth and roped together. Here the Scots spearmen were formed into four great masses, known as schiltrons, of circular form and ready to face outwards in any direction. The spearmen, when ready for action, would level their long pikes from the hip to repel cavalry; the immediate front ranks would kneel on the right knee, against which the butt of the spear was placed; thus a bristling wall of sharp spear-points presented itself in whatever direction the cavalry might choose to attack. Between each of the schiltrons was placed a band of the Ettrick archers, whilst the cavalry remained close at hand in reserve.

On the morning of the battle Edward had to be painfully assisted in mounting his horse; during the previous night, whilst sleeping with his men on the bare heath alongside their chargers, he had been trodden on by the horse, so that three ribs were broken. Patched up by the surgeons, he laboriously but resolutely mounted and showed himself to his troops. He ordered the banners to be unfurled, the trumpets to sound, and the army rolled forward towards the forest of Falkirk. On reaching the summit of the heights of Callendar, the whole English army halted; at their feet lay the fertile carse of Falkirk, and the vast oak forest known as the Torwood stretched away to where the towers and town of Stirling rose in the sunshine. The river Forth flowed like a thread of blue and silver between forests in all the glorious foliage of summer. In the immediate foreground, midway between Falkirk and the river of Carron, the weapons of the Scots army gleamed and twinkled in the sun's rays.

The English army celebrated Mass, conducted by the Bishop of Durham clad in full armour with a sword by his side and a shield slung at his back. The array that surrounded the militant churchman was impressive – the banners bore the arms of Edward . . . gules, three lions passant regardant; and those of St Edward the Confessor – a cross fleury between five martlets or. The tunics worn over the mail shirts were elaborately painted and blazoned; those curious ornaments called ailettes were worn on the knights' shoulders. The barrel-shaped helmets were surmounted by their crests; skull-caps, spherical and conical, were worn by the infantry; the lances had little emblazoned banners hanging from their heads. The Scots' banners showed the Scottish lion rampant, and the silver cross of St Andrew; Wallace himself wore a helmet surmounted with a dragon crest.

Then, as had been ordered, the English army advanced in three columns of horsemen, with the archers disposed between them. The first column was led by the Earl Marshal; the second by the fighting Bishop of Durham and the third by Edward in person. The mediaeval knight seldom took the trouble to examine the ground over which he was to fight, consequently the first column, riding furiously forward, dashed pell-mell into the marsh. The heavily armoured men and horses floundered wetly in the morass, English and Gascon alike, whilst the Scots archers poured arrows into them and caused considerable casualties. The rearmost ranks of the column, seeing the danger, swerved to their left to find firmer ground, then, closing their files, crashed into the Scots formations. Wallace looked around him and cried loudly:

'Now! I haif brocht ye to the ring – hop gif ye can!'

The unwavering barrier of outstretched spears in the hands of sturdy and resolute Scots brought the knights of the first column to a shuddering halt, so that they milled, cavorted and plunged across the front of the position as they tried to force their way through, reaching out to strike at the dismounted Scots before them. Seeing the error of the first column, the Bishop of Durham's second group avoided the marsh and wheeled to the right so that they threatened the Scots' left flank.

57

The small body of Scots cavalry eyed with some misgivings the approach of this vastly superior mounted force and wavered, then a few turned and fled, panic set in and the whole force fled from the field without striking a blow; a disaster later reputed to have been due to the treachery of their leader, Comyn.

Notwithstanding this, the Scots infantry remained steady and unbroken, presenting a threatening and ominously unwavering front. The experienced Bishop saw that this was the Welsh hedgehog all over again and realised that it would be prudent to wait until the archers came up with the King's division. He halted his force and they sat looking at the grim Scots formation; after a few minutes Radult Basset de Drayton, for a time the English governor of Edinburgh Castle, scornfully bellowed:

'Stick to thy mass, thou Lord Bishop! We shall conduct the military operations of this day!'

The Bishop bridled – brandishing his sword, he cried:

'On then, for this day we are all bound to do our duty as good soldiers!'

Spurring his horse, he led his column ponderously towards the enemy, to fall heavily on the Scots left whilst the remnants of the Earl Marshal's column assailed their right. The Scottish pikemen stood firm, shoulder to shoulder; again came the milling, scuffling and plunging of injured horses as knights bumped and got into each other's way but without forcing the position at any point. The English horsemen drew back, their horses breathing heavily. They gathered themselves and charged again . . . and again . . . and again . . . but they still had not broken through the levelled pikes when the King came up, leading the infantry and the remainder of the cavalry around the end of the marsh. He took in the situation at a glance; brought his archers forward so that they were within point-blank range of the Scots masses, a manoeuvre made possible because the Ettrick archers with their leader, the young Knight of Bonhill, had all been killed or had fled when ridden down by the English cavalry.

At the King's orders, the archers concentrated their rain of arrows on particularly stubborn points of Scots resistance; a hail of clothyard shafts poured unceasingly into the unarmoured ranks of the Scots, mercilessly bringing them crashing to the ground. Very soon the 'wood of spears' began to waver, to become thinner and less threatening as man after man dropped to the ground with an arrow projecting from his unprotected body. Deserted by their cavalry and their own archers destroyed, the Scots infantry levelled their pikes over a breastwork of their own dead and dying as they made desperate attempts to hold their ground. But their numbers were thinning fast and they were becoming unsteady; their morale was wavering as they lost heart at the hopeless prospect of fighting against the hissing death that came at them from beyond their reach. Here and there a man crept away from the formations, soon the trickle became a stream and disorder became evident.

Seeing that the moment was ripe, Edward threw in the cavalry of his own division; they thundered across the torn ground in a sudden charge, to dash through the gaping ranks of Scots pikemen and to lumber through the scattered ranks laying about them with lance, sword and axe. Once inside the pikes, there was nothing to stop the knights; they wallowed in a dreadful slaughter of their lighter-armed enemy. Fighting bravely, wielding his great two-handed sword, Wallace slugged his way from the field accompanied by a handful of faithful followers. His army was shattered and of those who escaped the shambles many were drowned crossing the river Carron in headlong flight to the north.

To the defeated Scots there was the minute consolation that before being vanquished they had come within sight of victory; the monumental stubbornness of the schiltrons had proved a match for cavalry charges far more violent than anything seen in the Welsh wars. In spite of the fact that archers supplemented by cavalry had proved that they could beat such tactics, the formation tried out by the Welsh and perfected by Wallace was to be the basic method of infantry fighting up to the early nineteenth century at Waterloo, outlasting the heavy-armed cavalry and long surviving the introduction of firearms.

Falkirk was the first engagement of any real size or importance in which archers, properly supplemented by cavalry, played a leading part. So striking was the demonstration of the devastating effect of the longbow that no English commander could fail to be impressed or to see the tactical lesson that had been set out before him.

8

Bannockburn – 1314

The Battle of Bannockburn has figured so much in legend and story that it is difficult to disentangle what actually took place; still more difficult to discover is *where* it took place. Many antiquarians have lost their tempers over its true acreage, but the actual site seems to have been within the angle of Bannockburn and the river Forth, just to the south-east of Stirling, in the parish of St Ninians. The details of this – 'the most lamentable defeat which an English army ever suffered' – are similarly blurred, but out of the confusion arises the claim that it is . . . 'the only pitched battle in recorded mediaeval history in which infantry totally and overwhelmingly defeated cavalry'.

In the summer of 1314 King Edward II – the vacillating son of an inspiring father – invaded Scotland. Robert Bruce withdrew to the Forth, knowing that Edward would tire his troops and strain his commissariat in crossing the wasted lands to the south. Stirling Castle, commanding the only bridge over the river, was being besieged by the Scots and Edward was determined to relieve it. He had to move quickly because, by an arrangement common in mediaeval warfare, the defenders had agreed to surrender if no relief arrived by midsummer's day.

Bruce gave a lot of thought to his selection of a position on which to give battle to the numerically superior English. He had to bear in mind his great deficiency of cavalry, those few he had, both in numbers and accoutrements, being totally unfitted to cope with the English men-at-arms. Both from his own experience and that of Wallace, he was aware that a body of Scots infantry, when armed with their lengthy pikes and judiciously posted, could effectively resist all charges of cavalry. The piece of ground that Bruce selected was then known as the New Park, partly open and partly encumbered with trees; on one side it was protected by a morass, the Newmiln Bog, the passage of which he knew to be difficult and dangerous. In his rear lay a little valley above which rose a long green ridge, now known as the Gillies Hill, for thereupon were all his camp-followers and baggage.

Bruce received tidings on the 22nd of June 1314 that the English were advancing from Edinburgh. He immediately marched his men, about 8,000 in all, from the Torwood to the positions that he had assigned to them less than two days before. He formed them in four columns of divisions, apart from each other yet near enough to keep in touch. The right column was commanded by his brother Edward; the left by Douglas and the young Steward of Scotland; the centre by Thomas Randolph, the veteran Earl of Moray; and the reserve or fourth column was commanded by Bruce himself. He had a small body of cavalry, under Sir Robert Keith, the Mareschal of Scotland; to them he assigned the important and specific duty of attacking and, if possible, dispersing the English archers.

The Scots dispositions had been made to meet an attack along the old Roman road which ran from Falkirk to Stirling; this meant that Bruce's three columns were facing south-east, the direction by which he expected the English to approach. The Scots were in a line extending from the brook, or 'burn', called the Bannock, to the village of St Ninian. The right wing was protected by means of pits dug where the ground was firm, about three feet deep with a stake in each, lightly covered with sods and branches. Iron calthrops – triangular metal pieces constructed in such a manner that a point sticks threateningly upwards whilst the other points rest on the ground – were strewn over areas where cavalry might be expected to charge, so that their horses would be lamed by the sharp points.

Edward's army moved throughout the morning and early afternoon of 23rd June, being already weary when they came into the Scots' sight as they debouched from the vast wood which then stretched away towards Falkirk. The June sunshine fell brightly on their burnished arms, innumerable white banners were fluttering in the slight breeze and the particoloured pennons of the knights floated above the glittering columns like a vivid sea. Edward obviously considered that his first objective was to contact Stirling Castle in force, so that he could release its commander, Sir Robert Mowbray, from his promise of surrender. That done, the garrison could then, without dishonour, make a sortie on the Scottish left wing. To accomplish the task, Edward sent forward a force of about 500 cavalry under Sir Robert Clifford; they made a great circuit by the low grounds bordering on the Forth and had actually passed the Scots' left before Bruce detected the glitter of their spears and armour arising through the long line of dust that rolled northward in the direction of Sitrling.

It is not clear whether the English force came up against the Scots defences or whether Bruce sent out a strong party to counter them; but it does seem apparent that the cavalry were repelled by the Scottish spearman and sent reeling back in complete disorder, horses galloping in all directions with empty saddles.

Whilst this affair took place, the English vanguard were still steadily advancing, but yet so distant that Bruce, who had not mounted his battle-charger, was still riding along his line mounted on a small hackney, to see that all were in their places. He carried a battleaxe in his hand, and wore a golden crown upon his helmet thus showing to all that he was the King. From the English vanguard there came galloping 'a wycht knicht and hardy' named Sir Henry de Bohun, who bravely conceived the idea of terminating the strife at once and covering himself with honour. Couching his lance, he rode furiously at the King.

Armed at all points and more heavily mounted, the encounter was most unequal but Bruce did not decline it, and rode forward to meet him in full career. Just as they were about to close he swerved his hackney round, and as de Bohun's lance passed harmlessly, he clove his head and helmet in twain with one blow of his battle-axe, and laid him dead at his feet. The weapon was shivered by the violence of the stroke; and to those who blamed him for his temerity, Buce replied simply:

'I have broken my good battle-axe.'

Easily discouraged, Edward now decided to try to outflank the Scots, turning their position under cover of darkness. So the English spent the night of 23rd/24th June following the course of the little river Bannock, which joins the Forth a few miles below Stirling, and crossing it in the marsh flats between Bannockburn village and Crookbridge. In the fourteenth century this area was extremely wet and marshy, making it a very difficult passage for heavy cavalry; the 20,000 heavily armed men of Edward's army spent all night laboriously crossing the stream. The sun rises early on midsummer day in Scotland and daybreak found the English host a disorganised mass milling about on the marshy flats below St Ninian's Church. The main English body was across the stream but not yet formed up for battle; only the vanguard under the Duke of Gloucester had managed to get into any sort of order.

They were given no time to organise; Bruce saw that this was the one occasion in a thousand when his pikemen could, in attack, be more than a match for Edward's cavalry. Rapidly facing his army to the new front, he launched them down the

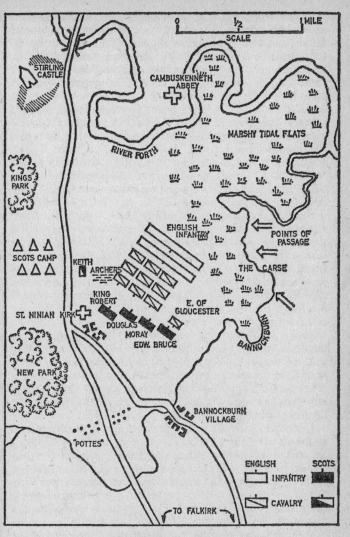

Battle of Bannockburn
24th June 1314

slight slope in echelon of schiltrons. In the white light of the early morning the still floundering English cavalry suddenly became aware of the phalanxes of pikes threateningly in motion and bearing down upon them. Before they could gather themselves, the footmen crashed heavily into the wallowing mass of men and horses; the great clash of men and arms at the first shock was said to have been heard over some distance. The attack had a devastating effect, many of the cavalry were immediately unhorsed to roll helplessly on the ground, while their horses, stabbed and maddened with wounds, plunged, reared and bolted, to spread confusion to the rear.

Warned by the noise, some of the English archers nimbly ran forward to a position on the right flank of the affray, getting their unarmoured persons out of trouble and also causing casualties in the massed Scots ranks. For a short time they fired unchecked, their arrows carving the usual deadly gaps in the hitherto steady Scots ranks. Sad experience had already warned the Scots that this might occur; the mounted force under Sir Robert Keith, that had been reserved for this very purpose by Bruce, came swiftly round the fringes of the morass and thundered into the lightly clad archers. Lacking spears or other long weapons and without any heavy support, the archers were immediately overthrown as they huddled together; soon they had been cut down or dispersed in all directions, further adding to the disorder that was now turning the English army into an undisciplined rabble. Seeing what had happened, other English archers feared to move to the flanks and tried to make their presence felt by firing from the rear, but their flights of arrows, discharged over the heads of their own troops against targets out of their sight, did little damage to the Scots and probably far more to the struggling English cavalry.

The battle developed into a confused mêlée between Bruce's spearmen and the English men-at-arms; the huge masses of horse and foot stood locked together. The English cavalry tried desperately to extricate themselves but were quite unable to find sufficient space to draw out and charge back in. Fresh knights coming up from Edward's main body could only make partial and ineffective charges in small bodies, efforts which failed utterly to break down the line of pikes, which caused dreadful casualties to the cavalry. The air was filled with the din of war, the clang of arms, the shouting of warcries; horses ran masterless, banners alternately rose and sank while the ground ran with blood amid the shreds of armour, broken spears, pennons and rich trappings torn and soiled with blood and muddy clay.

The Scots were pressing hard on the wavering masses of the English, whose rear ranks found it impossible to get up and into the fray; they stood helpless whilst their comrades were mown down. Then the English line began to give way, to falter; the gaps became larger as the exhausted and dispirited men looked wildly about them and wavered. Suddenly, like a dam before a tidal wave, it broke completely. The men who had not fallen on the pikes turned and fled in disorder. The panic was contagious, affecting those behind them who had not even had the opportunity of lifting their arm to make a warlike stroke; they stared hopelessly at the fleeing front ranks and then turned to fly with them, running for their lives until the defeat became a rout. Behind them lay the marshy banks of the Bannockburn and the broad reaches of the river Forth – they had no easy road to freedom. Soon, the narrow ravine of the burn was literally choked and bridged over by the slain; they piled up at the obstacle it presented until, coupled with the difficult nature of the ground, which held up the fugitive horsemen, the Scottish spearmen were upon them. Many, in terror, dashed their mounts into the river Forth where they drowned miserably.

Leaving the remnants of his army to their fate, Edward eluded capture by taking a circuitous route which led him past Stirling Castle; here he asked for shelter, but the Governor refused to admit him and shortly afterwards surrendered the castle as he had promised. The defeated King struggled on until he reached the castle of Dunbar, where he was hospitably received by the Earl of March. Compared with the slight losses of the Scots, the English army had lost an enormous number of men. The lesson standing out for all to learn was that cavalry, no matter how brave or determined, cannot defeat steady pikemen, unless the horsemen are supported by archers, who, in their turn, are worthless without the backing of heavy troops. Bannockburn was an exceptional reverse to the usual and fast developing successful methods of the English, but it was a battle lost by unskilful, almost insane, generalship rather than by failing to use the tactics that had brought victory at Falkirk.

9

Halidon Hill – 1333

With the notable exception of Bannockburn, for the two centuries that followed the Battle of Falkirk, its characteristics were almost monotonously repeated whenever Scots and English met in battle. Only in smaller forays did the Scots leaders, in the same way as the Welsh before them, manage to evade and draw the enemy into their unknown and difficult country so that their unmounted spearmen could bring disaster to the heavily armoured English knight. With these almost insignificant exceptions, the battles of Halidon Hill, Neville's Cross, Homildon and Flodden were all variations on the same theme. The steady but slow-moving masses of the Scottish infantry fell a sacrifice to their own persistent bravery as they staggered forward in vain attempts to reach the well-chosen position lined by archer-flanked men-at-arms. The English bowman might well boast that he carried twelve Scots lives at his girdle; he had but to launch his shaft into the easy target presented by the great surging mass of pikemen and it was certain to do dreadful execution.

In 1333 King Edward III of England decided to aid Edward Baliol in his attempt to wrest the Crown of Scotland from the young King David II, a minor who ruled with the aid of a Regent. The capture and reduction of the town of Berwick was Edward's first objective; with a powerful army he laid siege to the town, investing it by land and sea. Following the slaughter of a number of Scots hostages before the walls of the town, the Governor, Sir William Keith, gave one of the conditional surrender promises characteristic of the time. He agreed unconditionally to surrender before the hour of vespers on the 19th of July unless the Scots, in the meantime, could reinforce the garrison with 200 men-at-arms, or defeat the English in a pitched battle. To prevent the loss of this important frontier town, the Scottish army, under the Regent, crossed the Tweed on the 18th of July and encamped at Dunse Park, a few miles north of Berwick.

The Scots leader – Archibald Douglas, Lord of Galloway – was a brave man but an imprudent leader. He had heard but failed to observe the dying advice of King Robert: '. . the fate of the kingdom should never, if possible, depend upon the doubtful issue of a general engagement.' Douglas determined on just such a course of action, apparently confident that both he and his army would be victorious. He found the English strongly positioned on the crest of an eminence called Halidon Hill, situated to the westward of the town of Berwick. Little is known of the specific nature of the English position or their dispositions, save that Baliol commanded one of the wings and that a marshy hollow lay in front of their line.

The first of the four columns into which the Scottish army was divided was led by John, Earl of Moray, assisted by John and Simon Fraser of Oliver Castle; the second by the Steward of Scotland, a boy of sixteen years but assisted by his uncle, Sir James Stewart; the third was led by Douglas himself, having with him the Earl of Carrick, and the fourth column, in reserve, was led by Hugh, Earl of Ross. The numerical strength of the Scots army is variously recorded by the historians. It is believed to have been larger than the English, and the Continuator of Hemingford, a contemporary chronicler, gives it as 14,655 fighting men. These consisted of 55 knights, 1,100 mounted men-at-arms, and 13,500 lightly armed foot soldiers.

It was noon on the 19th of July 1333 when this force moved forward to decide the fate of Berwick, and possibly Scotland. They received an early set-back when they came up to the English position, finding that it was posted in such a way as to be impossible to attack with cavalry. The whole of the Scottish knights and men-at-arms therefore dismounted, sent their horses to the rear with their pages and prepared to fight on foot. The order was given to advance and the force ponderously lurched forward; up the slope of Halidon Hill they plodded, heads down and sheltered by their upraised forward shoulder. Nevertheless they were severely galled by the fierce fire of the English archers. In spite of this, they managed to reach the marsh, spreading before the the English position without losing their order, but here the disasters of the day began. The soft, boggy ground exacted its toll upon the heavily clad men, impeding them and slowing them down so that the stronger pressed forward and the weaker lagged back and the ranks became broken. All the time, without cessation, the archers poured in their volleys from the crest of the hill; they fired with certain aim and fatal effect at such close range. An ancient writer, quoted by Tytler, says: 'These arrows flew as thick as motes in the sunbeam.'

The struggling Scots began to fall in their dozens, scores and then hundreds; but the still-strong survivors battled their way through the marsh to struggle laboriously and wearily forward. Their long pikes held in front of them, levelled points unwavering, they gained encouragement from the now-nearness of the English. Mustering their strength, they made a furious uphill charge. The impact was noisy and breathtaking, so furious was it that the English line momentarily wavered and stepped back, It was, however, only as if they had stepped back in admiration of the strength and courage of the Scots, whom they now found to be breathless and disordered by their climb and struggle through the marsh so that their fighting was but briefly fierce and spasmodic. The ill-fated and ill-led Scots were unable to sustain their initial impetus and in a short and sharp struggle were remorselessly borne back in a slow pageant of desperately struggling men, to be finally forced back into the deadly embrace of the cloying marsh.

The Earl of Ross led the reserve to attack the wing of the English army led by Baliol, but he was soon killed and the attack petered out. Fighting in the van, Douglas received a mortal wound and was captured, together with the Earls of Sutherland and Monteith. The Scots now were beginning to give way on all sides; to make matters worse, the pages at the foot of the hill, seeing the day going against their masters, panicked and fled with the horses; the weary knights and men-at-arms now had no means of escape as they were too spent to run far in their armour. This meant that very few of the nobles or men-at-arms escaped in the bloody pursuit that followed; it only ended when 4,000 or more Scots lay dead on the slopes of Halidon Hill and in the fields around it. English historians of the day claim that the English lost only one knight, one esquire and twelve foot soldiers.

'Nor will this appear incredible,' said Lord Hailes, 'when it is remembered that the English ranks remained unbroken and that their archers, at a secure distance, incessantly annoyed the Scottish infantry.'

The town and castle of Berwick surrendered on the 20th of May, according to the agreement.

After the dust had died down at Bannockburn, nineteen years before, it was realised that it need never have been such a dreadful defeat; that the English possessed the tactical combination to destroy the advance of the Scottish spearmen. In the years between Bannockburn and Crécy there was a decisive difference, a difference ably exploited at Halidon Hill. It was a tactic that utilised the old method of receiving the enemy's attack by dismounted men-at-arms drawn up to exploit the advantages of mass and density, coupled with the innovation of having archers drawn up on the flanks to inflict maximum damage on the advancing enemy before he could come to grips. As early as 1322, Andrew Harcia, fighting for Edward II, had used archers and dismounted men-at-arms when disputing the passage of the river Ure with Thomas of Lancaster and the Earl of Hereford. Ten years later Edward Baliol, invading Scotland to claim the throne, stood on the defence on Dupplin Moor; the shooting of his archers from the flanks enabled his dismounted centre to win the day. Halidon Hill, in 1333, gave Edward III the opportunity of practising the same tactics but with greater elaboration; the King was soldier enough to know what he had at his disposal.

The means had been devised to overthrow the schiltrons – if the Scottish spearmen stood firm they were decimated by archery until the English men-at-arms came into the assault. If the Scots attacked they were beaten by dismounted men-at-arms, flanked by archers. In these early years of Edward III the essential military conditions of success in the Hundred Years War, both in tactics and in organisation, had already been prepared.

10

The Archer at Sea: Sluys – 1340

The English victories over the Scots seem to have made no impression whatsoever upon those responsible for military affairs in France. As though to give the French a last chance of assessing the new English tactics by parading before them in victory the archers, the backbone of the successful methods, the opening notes of the long Anglo-French conflict rang out first over water. Philip of France was well aware of Edward's designs on his throne and, as part of his preparations, he gathered together a large fleet of Norman and Genoese ships-of-war. These he assembled in Sluys harbour, from where they could emerge to cut communications with the English fleet when they made for Antwerp or ports of Flanders.

Hearing of this, Edward collected from ports both in the north and south of his kingdom a fleet to face the French; numbers on both sides are greatly at variance in the different chronicles, some going so far as to state that the French had 400 vessels to the English 260 sail – at least the proportionate sizes are probably correct! Edward in person commanded the English fleet, which was fought by 4,000 men-at-arms and 12,000 archers – large numbers of men for the time. The English appeared off Sluys on the 24th of June 1340; they entered the harbour at about noon when the tide was high, to see the French ships in four lines, bound and clamped together with ropes and chains to form four gigantic floating platforms. Sea battles, being contested by land armies, had to have battlefields.

Edward displayed that genius for the art of war which always characterised him, giving the necessary orders and forming his lines as if he had been bred to the sea. The English ships formed into two lines, the first consisting of the largest and stoutest ships to bear the brunt of the encounter, each alternate ship being filled with archers, supported by men-at-arms. The second line was almost a reserve, to be drawn upon if necessary. The English line-up was literally a 'Crécy-formation' on the high seas.

Each English vessel clamped itself by grappling-irons to its opposite French number, until the harbour resembled a vast floating raft of fighting ships. At such close range the archers had 'sitting targets' and their arrows whirred in a deadly sleet among the massed ranks on the French decks. The bowmen were shooting at a range which was so short as to enable a cloth-yard shaft to pierce through mail coats or transfix a shield, even if it were an inch thick. When they closed at first, the English could see the French ships' decks crowded with massed figures, waving arms, exultant faces; in a few minutes it had been replaced with a blood-soaked shambles, with bodies piled three-deep upon each other, the living cowering behind the dead to shelter themselves from the sudden storm-blast of death. With the enemy dead piled high, the English men-at-arms warily clambered across the gap between the vessels and on to the French decks, to mingle with the enemy so closely that it was impossible for the archers to draw string to help them. It was a wild chaos where axe and sword rose and fell, dagger and pike lunged and pierced home; Englishman and Frenchman staggered and slipped on decks cumbered with bodies and slippery with blood. The clang of blows, the cries of the stricken, the short deep shouts of the men-at-arms and the archers, who had dropped their bows and entered the mêlée with swords and mauls, rose together in a deafening tumult.

Remorselessly, the English men-at-arms carried on the slaughter begun by the archers, slowly but decidely they pushed their opponents across the treacherous decks, step by step, until they plummeted into the sea below – to sink like stones in their armour. Others rushed with wild screams and curses, diving under the sails, crouching behind booms, huddling into corners like rabbits when the ferrets are upon them, as helpless and as hopeless. They were stern days, and the ordinary soldier, too poor for a ransom, had no prospect of mercy upon the battlefield, even when it was at sea.

Only the rear squadron of twenty-four French ships escaped, the remainder being captured or destroyed. Edward personally claimed that 30,000 French had been killed, but a more reasonable estimate would be something like 10,000 or 12,000; the English lost about 4,000 and one great ship, a galley from Hull, was sunk with all hands by a shower of stones, a somewhat singular broadside but common in those days.

Edward kept at sea for three days with all his banners flying, to put his victory beyond all dispute. It is recorded that only one man in France dared tell King Philip the terrible story of the loss of his fleet – the court buffoon, who exercised the traditional licence given to the fool. Coming into the King's presence in an apparent passion, he exclaimed: 'Cowardly Englishmen! Dastardly, faint-hearted Englishmen!' Philip enquired why he so called them. 'Because,' replied the jester, 'they durst not leap out of their ships into the sea, as the brave Frenchmen did!'

'The name of Edward III,' says Sir Harry Nicolas, 'is more identified with the naval glory of England than of any other of her sovereigns; for though the sagacious Alfred and the chivalrous Richard commanded fleets and defeated the enemy at sea, Edward gained in his own person two signal victories, fighting on one occasion until his ship actually sank under him, and was rewarded by his subjects with the proudest title ever conferred on a British monarch – "King of the Sea". '

The victory at Sluys seems to have so raised the ardour of the English parliament that they were eager for the prosecution of the war and gave Edward every possible aid.

Another foretaste of what was to come occurred when Edward sent Sir Walter Manny with a small force to raid the Flemish island of Cadzand; this was a reprisal for a French raid on Portsmouth and the South Coast. There is quite a modern flavour about this small action in which the archers were used as 'artillery' to cover an infantry landing. Froissart writes: 'The archers

71

were ordered to draw their bows stiff and strong and set up their shouts; upon which those who guarded the haven were forced to retire, whether they would or not, for the first discharge did great mischief, and many were maimed or hurt.' Landing under cover of the arrow-barrage, the infantry then formed up in line with the archers massed in two bastions at the ends of the line. This later-to-become-familiar formation achieved a signal success and the archers had ushered in the long, long war.

11

Morlaix – 1342

The longbow had as yet been employed principally in defensive warfare and against an enemy inferior in cavalry to the English. But when Edward III led his invading force into France the conditions of war were entirely changed for the English. Now they were up against a country to be invariably superior in the numbers of their horsemen, so while the tactics of the archer were to remain defensive, they also had to be varied to meet the new threat. But the yeoman with his longbow was soon to find that the charging squadron presented an even better mark for his shaft than the stationary mass of infantry formed by the Scots schiltron. At the beginning of the Hundred Years War, in the early 1340's, the Continental world had not yet learned that it was almost hopeless for cavalry to try to force, in a frontal attack, a position defended by men-at-arms supported on their flank by archers.

The French had learned nothing from what had already transpired in Scotland and at Sluys and Cadzand; in fact they learned nothing from the battles that were to follow and were still making the same mistakes eighty years later! When the now well-tried technique was used in a battle near Morlaix in 1342, a few years before Crécy, it seems to have taken the French completely by surprise, as it did a short space of four years later on the fatal field of Crécy.

Morlaix was the first pitched land battle of the Hundred Years War; it proved that Bannockburn and Halidon Hill had taught the English something. In fact Halidon Hill formed the prototype for

Morlaix and all the other great battles of the war – except the last. The Earl of Northampton, with an army of about 3,000, was besieging Morlaix in September 1342; he was suddenly threatened by a relieving army of between 15,000 and 20,000 under Charles de Blois. Realising that he must not permit his army to be caught between Charles on the one side and the town on the other, Northampton marched out to find a suitable position in which he could accept battle. He was looking for a ridge or hill which would allow of a position with a forward slope giving a long view to the front, preferably striding the road upon which the enemy was expected to approach. If he had a wood in his rear, then it was ideal, for the position could not be effectively flanked by cavalry and the wood was a useful baggage-park.

On the road to Lanmeur, about four miles from Morlaix, he found what he sought – a position astride the road on the beginning of a gentle slope into a dip about 300 yards in front, with a wood immediately in rear of the position. The English line, about 600 yards in length, was about 50 yards in front of this wood, with a trench dug about 100 yards from the wood. Taking a lesson from the 'pots' of the Scots at Bannockburn, the English covered the trench with grass so that it served as a booby-trap for the enemy horsemen. The English men-at-arms were dismounted and in the centre of the line, with the archers stationed on the flanks. The Count of Blois drew up his army in three huge columns, one behind the other with a space between each; the leading column, formed of local levies, being dismounted.

The French advanced straight down the hill, into the slight dip and up the other side towards the waiting English. As soon as they were within range, the column was sent reeling back down the hill by a hail of arrows; they did not even reach the hidden trench. The second column, of mounted men, were launched at the English; they rode forward colourfully, impetuously and unsuspectingly, to plunge into the hidden trench in a tangled confusion of horses and men. Here they were bedevilled and distracted by arrows as they tried to sort themselves out and get back into some sort of order; but the attack had lost its momentum, it had come to a halt. With the exception of about 200 horsemen who did go forward and reach the English line, to be killed or captured, the second attack dribbled back.

Now a pause ensued, whilst the French licked their wounds and considered their next course of action. Northampton prayed that they would retreat, but to his dismay they showed no signs of this and he could see their third column, bigger than his whole army, drawn up on the ridge facing him. The English commander knew that he was still in peril although he had already repulsed two columns each greater than his own small force. More worrying, his archers were desperately short of arrows and had no further source of supply. The third column showed signs of movement, it began ponderously to lurch forward. The English murmured in apprehension – they could see that the battered and almost filled-in trench would be of little aid to them on this occasion. Moreover, the French mass was large enough to extend beyond the English flanks and so threaten the position from the sides.

Northampton courageously decided upon a manoeuvre almost unprecedented for the era: he withdrew his force in order back into the shelter of the wood so that they formed a hedgehog or defensive line along the edges of the trees, facing in each direction. Reserving their scanty ammunition until the French came close, the English managed to prevent them from penetrating their new position at any point. Marksmanship was the order of the day and the droning of massed arrows was replaced by single 'whirrs' as individual shafts found their marks and, with a crash, a French man-at-arms would collapse from his startled horse.

Night was approaching, and the Count de Blois, discouraged and with his men deserting on all sides, began to withdraw slowly back to Lanmeur. Seeing this, Northampton gathered together his small band and, in a defensive formation, left the wood to return to the siege of Morlaix. He had the great satisfaction of knowing that he had achieved his purpose of setting to flight the relieving army, although it outnumbered him by four or five to one. But, more than that, he had perpetuated, knowingly it must be assumed, future tactics from the lessons learned at Bannockburn and Halidon Hill – the men-at-arms fighting dismounted, the trench in front forming an obstacle (a marsh at Halidon); the defensive position on a ridge, the skilful use of the archer's fire-power in co-operation with supporting heavy troops. All these factors co-ordinated to defeat the mounted attack, together making notable a battle claimed by those who fought in them all to have been even more desperately contested than Halidon Hill, Crécy or Poitiers.

The defeated Charles de Blois is again encountered in June 1346, when, with a force greatly superior in numbers, he came up with Sir Thomas Dagworth's small army at St Pol de Léon, north-west of Morlaix, on 9th June 1346. As at Morlaix four years previously the first attack of Charles was repulsed, then his second line came in to overlap the tiny English force on three sides. The English held their ground and poured in such deadly hails of arrows that the French were sent reeling back; after a little of this they fled from the field. There is no record that Charles was dismayed by the disastrous repetition, the further exhibition of the power of the English longbow coming just in time to add to the morale and prestige of the archers at Crécy.

PART THREE

THE YEARS OF VICTORY

12

Crécy – 1346

A brief note in records of the period indicates that Edward III was highly encouraged by such successes as Morlaix and that he was anticipating more battles in France. In 1342 he ordered that every sheriff must provide 500 white bow-staves and 500 bundles of arrows for the coming battles. The next year the order was repeated with the additional demand that the Sheriff of Gloucester was not only required to provide 500 white bow-staves but also the same number of painted staves. In the summer of 1346 Edward had marched his army from the Cherbourg Peninsula almost to Paris, crossing the Seine at Poissy and marching towards Amiens to make contact with his Flemish allies. But he found King Philip with a large army in the Amiens area, and they frustrated all Edward's attempts to take his army across the river Somme. Finally, by offering large rewards to prisoners, one Gobin Agache was persuaded to tell him of a practical ford at Blanchetaque (The White Spot). Here a man could cross the river, at low tide, with the water only up to his knees in spite of the ford being nearly 2,000 yards long.

It was essential that the English army should gain the far bank; their situation had suddenly become critical – boots were worn out, bread was scarce and the men were suffering from eating the unripe wayside fruit. Their horses were getting fewer in number and many knights were reduced to riding clumsy captured farm animals. Edward had no idea of the progress of his Flemish allies and he was out of touch with the fleet. The French army was vastly superior to the English force numerically, and Edward knew that he could easily lose the entire war in a single battle of a few hours' duration.

They reached the ford at dawn, when the tide was only just starting to ebb; they had four long and anxious hours to wait before the ford became crossable. They had marched in single column, Warwick leading the advance-guard with a force of archers, then men-at-arms, followed by baggage and, rearmost, the King's division. The column closed up until the entire army was concentrated on the south bank, immediately opposite the ford. It is said to have been ten o'clock before the first man – Hugh Despenser – led the vanguard of archers into the glistening water to begin what appeared to be an uneventful progress over the one-and-a-half-mile causeway. When they came within a hundred yards of the shore they were greeted with an unexpected shower of crossbow bolts – Philip had posted a force of about 3,500 men-at-arms and infantry, with a force of Genoese crossbowmen, to hold the ford.

Taken by surprise and without cover or protection, the English were massed in an easy target for the Genoese crossbows; they took a number of casualties as they tried to deploy and return the fire. The water was still waist-deep, making it difficult to wield the longbows efficiently, besides wetting the bowstrings. Both archers and cavalry stumbled and fell into the churned-up water as they were hit; some slipped off the causeway into the deeper river on either side. This causeway was wide enough for some eleven men to stand abreast, so the archers packed in whilst the remainder fired over the heads of the front rank. Quickly, the longbow assumed its habitual ascendancy over the crossbow and the Genoese fire began to slacken. Seeing this, Warwick gave the signal for the men-at-arms to advance; the horsemen plunged and splashed through and past the archers, who edged to the sides of the causeway to let them through. The English horse were met by some of the French cavalry who had plunged from the bank to dispute the passage and a confused, splashing conflict of short duration took place in the shallow water, ending with the French retiring in confusion to the bank. The English men-at-arms followed close behind them, the archers covering their advance with a steady barrage of hissing arrows. The French quickly showed that they wanted none of this and took flight, leaving behind them almost 2,000 casualties.

At the other end of the causeway, the last of the English men and wagons were entering the now rapidly deepening water. Suddenly the French advance-guard, under the King of Bohemia, came dashing up and there was a short, sharp engagement between them and the English rearguard. There were a few casualties and some wagons were captured, but the bulk of them, bearing their precious cargo of arrows, escaped and were trundling their way, axle-deep, across the river. The French made no attempt to pursue, allowing the English to escape – Edward had succeeded in crossing the river Somme and could now seek his Flemish allies and prepare a position in which to receive the French attack.

The English army marched to the edge of a forest about nine miles north-east of Blanchetaque and, on the day following the crossing, were halted on the banks of the little river Maye, beyond which lay a village called Crécy-en-Ponthieu. In this area Edward found a suitable position to offer battle: he chose a windmill-crowned ridge immediately to the north-east of the village, from which it extended for about 2,000 yards to the hamlet of Wadicourt. In front of the position was a depression, later to be called the Vallée aux Clercs (Valley of the Clerks), ranging from about one hundred feet in depth on the right to nothing on the left. The slope in front of the right flank of the position was about one in twelve and almost imperceptible on the left; the village and the river Maye protected the right flank against cavalry attack, but the left (and much weaker flank) had only the small hamlet of Wadicourt as protection, with open country beyond. A few hundred yards behind the centre of the ridge was a small wood, the Bois de Crécy-Grange.

Numerically, the English army is thought to have been between 12,000 and 13,000 strong, being positioned in three distinct divisions. That of the Black Prince, consisting of 800 dismounted men-at-arms flanked on either side by a total of 2,000 archers and about 1,000 Welsh spearmen, was placed well down the slope within 300 yards of the valley bottom. On the Prince's left and somewhat drawn back so that they were slightly higher up the slope, lay the rearguard under the experienced Earl of Northampton; it was smaller than the first division, consisting of about 500 men-at-arms and 1,200 archers formed up in the same manner. The right of this division rested on the Prince's left and its left flank was protected by Wadicourt. The third division, that of the King, consisted of 700 men-at-arms, 2,000 archers and perhaps 1,000 Welsh spearmen, and were formed on the plateau in front of the wood of Crécy-Grange, behind the battle of the Prince of Wales. The baggage was parked in a wagon-leaguer backing on to the wood; its interior being occupied by the horses and garrisoned by the pages, Edward intended to fight with his men-at-arms dismounted, as had been done by Northampton at Morlaix a few years previously. The Black Prince had as chief officers the Earls of Warwick and Oxford, and he was under the personal protection of Godfrey Harcourt.

The men-at-arms were deployed into line by the marshals and then a solid wedge of archers formed up on the flanks of each of

81

the divisions. Known as 'herces'[1] these wedges were formed by the body of archers inching forward diagonally, pivoting on the flank of their own men-at-arms; where the two contiguous lines of archers met, an apex was formed. In this way a bastion-like formation was created in the intervals between the divisions; obvious advantages being that the front of the men-at-arms *and* the flanks of the army could be enfiladed by arrow fire. The archers dug small holes in front of their position and planted a plentiful supply of arrows in the ground; their usual supply of twenty-four or forty-eight arrows being supplemented from the wagons. When they were exhausted, the archer had three choices:

1. He could await the arrival of a fresh supply from the wagons.

2. He could dash forward during a lull and pick up arrows fired at the enemy that had missed their mark and were lying on the ground. This was done at Poitiers.

3. He could abandon his bow and join in the mêlée with his sword, as he did at Agincourt. Being unencumbered with armour, the archers were more nimble and most effective in hand-to-hand fighting. They were probably hefty, muscular men, as only a strong man could effectively wield a long bow.

The men-at-arms were armour-clad; wearing a visored bascinet, the crested helmet was used only in the lists. The casing of the body in jointed armour was now nearly complete, and the adoption of breast and back plates enabled the knights to dispense with the ancient hauberk of rings. The use of plate-armour was a decided improvement from a protection point of view; it was also possibly lighter than chain mail with its accompanying garments. The magnificent jupon, emblazoned with the wearer's arms, and the splendid knightly girdle were both testimonies of the warlike age. Greaves, or jambs (steel boots) and sollerets to cover the feet had been introduced; the backs of the gauntlets were furnished with overlapping plates, armed with knobs or spikes of iron.

When every man in the army was in his allotted position, the King rode slowly down the line on a white palfrey; he studied the dispositions with an experienced eye and talked to the men, giving them words of cheer and encouragement. It was midday when he came to the end of the line, and there was still no sign of the French. Edward gave orders for the men to fall out and eat, positions to be instantly resumed at the sound of the trumpet. The men removed their helms, the archers laid their bows carefully alongside their arrows, so that they marked their places. When the food was consumed, the men lay down and rested or stood in

1. Meaning 'barrow' in Anglo-Saxon.

groups talking, eyes constantly straying in the direction from which the enemy was expected to come. Four o'clock came; still without any warning cry from the lookout at the top of the windmill. The sky suddenly darkened and a brief but fierce rainstorm fell upon them; the archers rushed to protect their precious bowstrings, each man quickly unstringing his bow and coiling up the string inside his hat. The storm passed over and the bows were re-strung; the clear air, fresh with the scent of the rain, hummed with the mumbling hubbub of thousands of deep male voices.

Above the noise came a sudden sharp cry from the windmill, which had been earlier picked as a post of command by Edward because of the clear view it gave of the whole position. The King rushed to verify that it did indeed betoken the approach of the enemy; satisfied, he gave the signal and the trumpets sounded. The groups broke up and dispersed; discarded armour and helms were hastily donned; everyone stood to their allotted post in grim and confident silence; they knew that everything was ready, that nothing had been overlooked. The archers had checked their distances and were conscious that their shafts could reach the bottom of the valley, but they were ordered to hold their fire until the enemy were within effective range. Then, with every man motionless and all eyes fixed forward, the van of the French army hove in sight, descending the gentle slope into the valley of the Maye. Their armour gleamed, and lance pennons fluttered; at first they seemed a formidable host but, as they moved nearer and with every step they took clearly seen from the English position, they lost much of their threat in the hour it took them to get within striking distance.

The French army had approached the battlefield from Marcheville, so that they had to turn sharply left to face the English position. The sudden change in the direction of march brought an inevitable disorder and the usually ragged march discipline of the French sadly accentuated the situation. It was a mixed army, formed of the King's regular troops; foreign notabilities with their contingents; German mercenaries and the Genoese crossbowmen, who had already tasted the power of English arrows. All were massed together with a disorderly, straggling crowd of provincial levies. Contingents jostled each other, units bumped and became inextricably mixed; the army was almost out of hand even before a shot had been fired. Testimony to this confusion are the varying reports on the size and disposition of the French army; its numbers are reported to have been as many as 145,000 or 100,000, its divisions from three to twelve. It seems from the more sober reports and chronicles that they were about three times as strong as the English army – consisting of about 40,000 men formed in three divisions. The first division consisted of about 6,000 Genoese crossbowmen under Antonio Doria and Carlo Grimaldi; the second was led by the Count d'Alençon, brother to the King, with three crowned heads serving under his banner – John of Luxemburg, the blind King of Bohemia; the King of the Romans, his son, and the King of Majorca. The third division was under Codemar de Faye.

King Philip was undecided as to his best course of action. He had been taken by surprise at the sudden sight of the English drawn up in battle array. His troops were wearied by the march, hungry and in considerable disorder; it seemed sensible to wait until the morning before attacking. He gave the order to halt. When the order reached the vanguard, the impulsive French knights at the head of the column believed that they were to be deprived of the honour of opening the battle, as they could see that some of the troops in the rear were still advancing. So they pushed forward impatiently, feeling confident that their superior numerical strength would triumph. Seeing them move forward, the main body persisted in following them until the whole army arrived so close to the English position that a battle became unavoidable. In pushing forward, the French knights forcibly propelled before them the Genoese mercenaries who formed the advance-guard. The heavily accoutred Italians, weary after a march of six leagues bearing their weighty weapons, drenched and draggled, conscious that they were virtually disarmed because of the wetness of their bowstrings, shuffled wearily into their stations along the French front. Seeing this hesitation and now being committed to fight, the King cried:

'Make the Genoese go in front and begin the battle, in the name of God and St Denis!'

The mercenaries muttered and complained to their constables:

'We be not well ordered to fight this day; we be not in the case to do any great deed of arms, and have more need of rest.'

The constables, in their turn, complained that their men were being unfairly treated. The Count d'Alençon was scornful:

'Truly, a man is well at ease to be charged with these kind of rascals, who are faint and fail us now when most at need!'

Stung by his words, the Genoese mercenaries attempted to deploy and march against the English position looming ahead of them. It was a difficult procedure for such a large body of already disordered men, now being rudely hustled in their rear

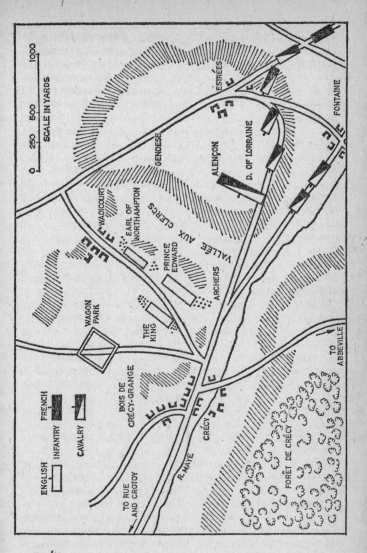

Battle of
Crécy

26th
August
1346

85

by the arrogant French knights. In spite of the efforts of these experienced professional soldiers, their line became hopelessly ragged and out of dressing, so that they had to be halted to re-form three times in less than a mile of shambling progress. In the rear of the English position, the sun emerged brilliantly, to shine full in the eyes of the enemy and to present conditions said to be ideal for the archers, now ominously testing their bows.

Slowly the Genoese continued their advance; their progress across the valley being marked with whoops, shouts and arm-waving as though to bolster up their flagging spirits. They halted, gave three ordered loud cries and then commenced to ascend the gentle slope leading up to the English position. The bolts they halted to occasionally discharge all fell short, the recent rain having sadly relaxed the strings of their clumsy weapons; their fingers fumbled as they went through the cumbrous process of winding up their arbalesta, their eyes fixed on the unmoving line to their front. When they came to within 150 yards of the English archers their forward movement wavered in the face of their silent, immobile foe; they set up more shouts and whoops in the hope of shaking that calm.

Ahead of the Genoese a sharp word of command rang out; in response the English archers, as one man, stepped forward a pace to draw their bowstrings to their ears. Suddenly the bright sunlight was shut off by black swarms of arrows, the air full of their hissing. The clothyard shafts quivered in the faces and bodies of the Italian mercenaries, the discharge striking their closely knit lines in devastating fashion. They reeled and staggered, falling into even greater disorder as they recoiled from the continuous shower of wailing arrows.

Their discomfort was increased by a series of belches of flame, with roaring noises like thunderclaps, followed by the hissing progress of heavy balls of iron and stone which tore through the ranks of the crossbowmen to prostrate men and stampede horses in the ranks behind them. It was Edward's 'secret weapon' – crude iron tubes that had been laboriously borne across France in the bottom of the ammunition wagons to take their place as the first cannon to be fired in open warfare. Surprising as their appearance must have been to the French, these crude and noisy innovations to the art of war do not seem to have had as much physical or morale effect upon the French as might have been expected. The chroniclers all continue to report this battle in the terms of devastating results of English archery rather than those caused by rough stone and iron balls, each of which weighed perhaps $1\frac{1}{2}$ to 2 lb. and were sent on their way with such a spectacular gush of flame and smoke.

The unfortunate, belaboured Genoese now had, crowding forward on their heels, the élite of the nobility of France, all spoiling for a fight and resentful that the foreign mercenaries had done them out of the honour of opening the battle. Like their leader, Count d'Alençon, they were ready to suspect the crossbowmen of treachery; had the Italians not baulked at going forward in the first place? The hot-headed d'Alençon provided the spark, crying loudly:

'Slay me those rascals! They do but hinder and trouble us without reason!'

Clapping spurs into his horse's flanks, he drove his charger into the midst of the Genoese, closely followed by his men-at-arms, shouting and cursing as they rode and trampled underfoot the mercenaries. Beset from both sides and unable to get close enough to the English to return their fire, the crossbowmen furiously discharged their bolts at their new adversaries, so that small internecine fights added to the confusion. The heavily armoured French knights were not to be withstood; they relentlessly battered their way forward towards the Prince of Wales's division, leaving behind them a trail of their own arrow-pierced knights and horses floundering among the crossbowmen they had ridden down.

In the meantime the divisions in the rear had also brushed past the luckless Genoese and deployed into position until a continuous line was formed roughly equal in length and parallel to the English position. Then began the series of fruitless charges of heavily clad horsemen lumbering uphill against showers of arrows remorselessly plaguing them; the great stallions, mad from the pain of the keen, barbed shafts, broke from all control. They pushed, reared, swerved and plunged, striking and lashing out hideously. Soon the ground was heaped with the bodies of men and horses. The men-at-arms forced their reluctant steeds forward, struggling on with heads bowed; the horses, belaboured with lengthy and fierce mediaeval spurs, were noisily shuffled towards the dismounted, armoured formations in front of them, whilst being assailed by a short-range crossfire of arrows from their flanks. As in almost every battle, the main assault of the French was directed against the dismounted men-at-arms rather than against the archers; a situation due mainly to the fact that they were 'channelled' that way in their efforts to get away from the hissing arrows. The Count d'Alençon and his remaining knights had reached and engaged in hand-to-hand fighting the battle of the Prince of Wales, whilst others had closed with Northampton's division. These were not concerted efforts but rather irregular and spasmodic surges that did not cause the English line to yield a single foot.

French casualties rose rapidly. The ground was heaped high with the bodies of men and horses. The Welsh and Irish foot soldiers now began to creep forward, bearing their great sharp knives. These men, clad in thick leather jerkins, nimble of foot and accustomed to a life of activity, mingled fearlessly among the confused masses of fighting men, creeping beneath the horses' bellies, standing up when they got a chance to stab horses and men. They slew by stabs and gashes through the joints in the armour those French men-at-arms, who rolled helplessly like turtles upturned amid the press.

The numerical superiority of the French enabled them to persist in their efforts, unsuccessful as they appeared to be up to then. Whenever a man fell, another lurched forward to take his place from the apparently inexhaustible supply of the French army. In this manner the pressure on the English line increased, particularly on the right, where Godfrey Harcourt began to feel anxious for the safety of his royal charge. In person, he ran clumsily across to the nearest unit of Northampton's division – that commanded by the Earl of Arundel – and begged him to put in a counter-attack, so striking in the flank those enemy assailing the Prince's division. Harcourt then sent a messenger to the King, asking for reinforcements. From his command-post high in the windmill, the King could see that Arundel's counter-attack was taking effect; that it was not yet the opportune moment to throw in his precious reserve. Without taking his eyes from the surging, heaving battle spread out before him like a colourful carpet, he said:

'Let the boy win his spurs,' waving his hand in dismissal as he spoke. The experienced soldier and King was right in his judgment. When the messenger arrived back, the Prince and his men-at-arms were sitting among the dead, resting after beating off the attack. In front of their position were more than 1,500 dead French men-at-arms.

In wave after wave, not continuously and with varying intervals, the French chivalry bravely and characteristically thundered clumsily up to the English position, without ever effecting a penetration before being beaten back. In the pauses the English archers would leave their lines, run forward to search for arrows among the dead. They did not waste time trying to pull them from the bodies of the dead, knowing that the barbed arrow-head could only be removed from soft flesh by major feats of surgery or extensive crude carpentry.

The old, blind King of Bohemia sat restlessly chafing on his charger, hearing all around him the noise of the battle. He repeatedly asked after its progress and then said:

'Sirs, ye are my men, my friends and companions. I require ye to lead me so far forward that I may strike one stroke with my sword.'

Two knights buckled the reins of their bridles to those of his horse, lest they should lose him in the press, and the three charged forward together. In the centre of them the old King held his sightless head high as though sniffing the scent of battle. The trio reached the fighting, guided their wrenching horses forward until they were brought up to a standstill by the press. The aged monarch swung a stroke with his sword, struck again – sometimes at thin air, sometimes feeling solid resistance that jarred his arm. They fought valiantly but perhaps ventured too far forward, to be found next day, still tethered to their King, about whom they lay dead.

The rearmost men, carried forward by their own momentum, surged on to the top of the foremost, to wedge the whole into a helpless, choking mass. Still the pitiless arrows hissed into the press and the entire French fighting line became a confused welter of struggling animals, maimed crossbowmen and fallen men-at-arms, who, crippled by the weight of their armour, lay an easy prey to the long, keen knives of the Welsh. It is reported that at least fifteen attacks were put in by the French, who did not realise in 1346 and still did not comprehend nearly 100 years later at Agincourt, that to force a line of bowmen supported by men-at-arms with a frontal attack was an almost hopeless task for cavalry. There is little that can be more disconcerting to charging cavalry than a flight of arrows, laying low not only many of the riders but also causing disorder by setting the wounded horses plunging and rearing so as to sadly check the impetus of the charge. Then, as the charge neared the English position, the wounds to man and horse became more numerous, the disorder increased, the pace progressively slackened until at last the charge came to a standstill, wavered and then withdrew.

The fight went on after darkness had fallen, under a rising moon, until late in the evening it petered out to give way to an uneasy semi-silence broken only by the groans of the wounded. Philip of France, with only three score knights remaining, was unwilling to believe that all was lost; he was prevented from personally leading yet another charge by the restraining hand on his horse's bridle of Sir John of Heynault, who said:

'Sire, depart while there is yet time. Lose not yourself willingly. If this field is lost, you shall recover it again another season.'

The English had won the day without stirring a foot from their position; the enemy had conveniently come to them to be killed. More than a third of his number lay dead before the unbroken English lines, the majority laid low by clothyard shafts. Wearied with slaughter and satiated with victory, the English lay down and slept, supperless, where they had fought. The Irish and Welsh infantry were out in full force, combing the battlefield and giving no quarter as they finished off those who had fallen but still lived. There was no attempt made to pursue the vanquished, who melted away silently into the night, each man retreating in whatever direction he fancied because there were few left to give commands or orders. King Philip had lost his own brother, the Count d'Alençon; his brother-in-law, John of Bohemia, and his nephew, the Count of Blois, besides a clean sweep of his generals. The flower of the chivalry of France had been wiped out, more than 1,500 of them, in a total casualty list of over 10,000. The rest of the army, the allies from Bohemia, Hainault and Flanders, dispersed and returned to their homes. In a few hours Philip, the most powerful monarch in Western Europe, had lost an army.

The next morning, Sunday, the 27th of August, arrived with a thick fog, as though mercifully to blanket the grim scene – the valley black with the bodies of men and horses. Edward sent his clerks out to make a tally of the dead, and, to this day, the scene of their labours is known as the Valley of the Clerks.

Before leaving the scene it might be opportune to consider why an overwhelming victory should have been gained by a force so much smaller in numbers than their enemy. Crécy proved that the archer, when supported by dismounted men-at-arms, could beat off the most determined cavalry charges. This was not news to Edward; he had learned much from Halidon Hill, Morlaix and other smaller battles, but probably even he was surprised at the way in which the battle had, for him, been so purely defensive. This is borne out by the fact that he had resisted using his reserve, even to aid his son; that he held them firmly under his hand, intending to launch them in a great, final counter-attack, a course of action made unnecessary by the desperate and senseless bravery of the French knights, who learned nothing

90

of what was happening from those who had charged before them and persisted in following the only creed they knew. In the end this resulted in the flower of French chivalry lying dead with arrows bristling from their bodies or awaiting the bloody knives of the Welsh and Irish.

Therein lay a lesson that the French never learned, refusing in their class-pride to recognise that their defeat was at the hands of despised peasants. For generations they persisted in the delusion that the defeat was due to the stability of dismounted English men-at-arms. In part this was true, because the newly successful English tactical scheme depended upon men-at-arms fighting dismounted and in mutual support of the archers. Undoubtedly, the qualities of the two armies had a great bearing on the result of the battle; on the one hand the English were well trained, well led, well disciplined and well armed. The French, on the other hand, were a hastily collected force from different countries, not articularly well trained and no unit knowing much about its neighbours. As a result it lacked cohesion, neither trusting nor respecting each other, so that, as an army, it was bound to disintegrate when exposed to ordered blows.

In this day and age it might seem incredulous that such a succession of fruitless charges should have been made when each one was obviously being decimated. Such a statement must be considered in the light of the happenings at Waterloo nearly 500 years later, when the cream of Napoleon's cavalry were wiped out in a succession of fruitless uphill charges against squares of British infantrymen, descendants of the archers of Crécy; or, even to the present day, within living memory are the vast and bloody onslaughts made on prepared positions by infantry during the war of 1914–18.

The Battle of Crécy marks a step in the progress of the military art, in the age-long contest between mounted and dismounted men, between missile and personal weapons and in the emergence of a third arm: artillery. It was a battle that should have taught a striking lesson to feudal chivalry, but the old tradition hallowing the mounted knight as the most honourable name in warfare was strong enough to be perpetuated for another century; the methods that really died on the 26th of August 1346 were still to be breathing in 1415 and even later. It would take more than one such disaster to destroy a system so intimately bound up with mediaeval life and ideas.

As an ironical epitaph to the French knight, it might well be said that his chivalrous code would have been horrified at the very thought of shirking a direct frontal attack against a numerically inferior enemy!

13

Neville's Cross – 1346

Following his defeat at Crécy and the melting-away of his army, Philip of France found himself sorely pressed by the invading army of Edward III. He sought to relieve this pressure by urgently entreating David II, King of Scotland, to invade England in the hope of drawing Edward back to defend his realm. David succumbed to the lure and, in October 1346, he marched his army over the border and into England, being assured that Edward and his chief commanders were absent so that '. . . here are none to oppose our progress save churchmen and base artisans'. He crossed the Tyne at Ryton, above the town of Newcastle, and advanced into Durham to encamp, on the 16th of October, at Beaurepair (Bear Park), about two miles north-west of the city of Durham.

Within the city itself, the utmost consternation prevailed; it appeared to be at the mercy of the invaders. But things were not as bad as they appeared and the Scots were to be opposed by a force that was collecting with all speed and considerable zeal. This army, well armed and numbering about 16,000 men-at-arms, archers and infantry, was led by the northern barons – Ralph, Baron Neville of Raby; Henry, Baron Percy of Alnwick; Musgrove, Scrope, Hastings and the ubiquitous Edward Baliol.

The English force advanced slowly and cautiously eastwards; near the village of Ferry Hill they met and scattered a raiding party of about 500 men under Sir William Douglas. The latter, flying from the field and leaving more than 200 of his force dead, arrived breathless at Beaurepair to warn David that the English had formed an army and were advancing to meet him. Still moving slowly by the Red Hills on the west of the city of Durham, the English were coming up to the ground on which the forthcoming battle was destined to be fought. The battle-field lay west and west by north of the cathedral; it was a level ridge, since cut up into fields and partly built over; northwards there was a sharp slope forming a kind of trough into which a spur juts out – hereabouts the ground was covered thickly by Shaw Wood. In the trough and woody recesses was a little pear-shaped hillock known as the Maiden's Bower, on the top of which the clergy from the city clustered to pray around the holy relic of St Cuthbert.

David formed the Scots army into three divisions. The first was led by the High Steward of Scotland, the second by the Earl of Moray and Sir William Douglas of Liddesdale (then named 'The Flower of Chivalry'), and the third division, consisting of select troops and a party of French auxiliaries, was led by the King in person.

The English were disposed so that Lord Percy led the vanguard which, in the battle, became the right wing and was opposed to the Scots left wing under the High Steward. The main body was commanded by Lord Neville and, as centre, in the battle joined issue with the Scottish main body and centre under King David. The English rearguard (the left wing) under Rokeby, was in conflict with the Scottish right wing led by the Earl of Moray. The English also had provided for that which the Scots had not – a powerful reserve of picked cavalry – mailed horsemen, under the command of Edward Baliol.

Still moving slowly, the English advanced and deployed for action; the Scots left their position on Durham Moor and moved forward to meet them. Sir John Graham, remembering how a quick cavalry movement against the archers at Bannockburn had decided the day, asked leave to attack them. 'Give me but one hundred horse and I shall disperse them,' he declared. King David refused and, at nine o'clock in the morning, ordered a general attack.

The Scots advance was sorely impeded by walls and hedges, behind each of which were stationed English archers, whose arrows galled and played the usual havoc with the advancing Scots. Flying as thick as hail, the destructive volleys, at long range, poured into the enemy so that their spearmen fell thickly without having been able to inflict a single injury upon the English. Graham, furious at this loss of men and sensible enough to realise that archers at 'long bowls' had a terrible advantage over men armed with sword, axe and spear, took matters into his own hands and struck the first blow. At the head of his own personal followers, he rode straight for the archers, charging down on them so quickly that his little band actually broke through in one place and dispersed the archers there. At short range,

Graham's horse was shot down and was wounded, but he managed to regain the Scots lines.

The High Steward, quickly grasping the situation, ordered his men to charge the partly disordered English right wing. Momentarily freed from the nagging arrows, the Scots came on with such impetuous fury that by sheer weight of sword and battle-axe they hurled the English column back in confusion against that of Lord Percy, whose wing was then in danger of rout. At this moment of crisis the value of possessing a cavalry reserve under a capable commander became apparent – Baliol, with great spirit, charged the Scottish troops threatening Percy. Not only was the Scots attack on the right wing repulsed, but that repulse was converted into a complete rout and within a brief space the division of the High Steward were a bunch of fugitives. The High Steward desperately worked to re-form and reorganise his troops, who were entangled among hedges and ditches, again being decimated by the fire of the now steady English archers.

The battle between the centres had been proceeding on almost equal terms. At a glance, Baliol took in the situation; refusing to succumb to the temptation of pursuing the beaten High Steward's division, he wheeled his men and flung them into a charge on the left flank of the Scottish King's division. The left flank of this formation, through the flight of the left wing, was left practically defenceless and Baliol's move proved almost completely disastrous to the Scots. Their centre, attacked in front by Neville (whose men had poured through gaps in the enclosures to charge the Scots in a somewhat confused but nevertheless desperate manner) and on the left flank by Baliol's cavalry, began to waver and slowly give way. The conflict was carried on relentlessly for some time, the English and the Scots hacking away at each other, the archers firing at whatever targets presented themselves and then laying on with their swords. In spite of the King, surrounded by his nobles, fighting bravely, his division began to break up, the fugitives taking off towards the right, where Rokeby was valiantly doing more than hold his own. But here the men of the Scots right division, hampered by the nature of the ground, could not retreat; caught in enclosures and between hedges, they were slain without mercy and died in heaps.

On all sides the Scots had now completely given way, but their King, by his exhortations and example, repeatedly brought masses of them back to the fray. It was in vain and at last, almost a precursor of Flodden, the remaining knights formed themselves in a ring around their monarch and stood at bay. In spite of their gallant defence, at noon the royal banner was seen to be beaten down; seeing it fall, the remnants of the Scottish army in all parts of the field fled in despair. Acknowledging that all was lost, the eighty or so knights remaining around David surrendered and, at last, the King himself was taken. His sword was broken in his hand and he was said to have had at least two severe body wounds, but proud, fiery and in the prime of life, David disdained captivity and tried to provoke his captor, Sir John Copeland, to kill him. Although he smashed his mailed gauntlet into that knight's face, his action did not bring the death he desired and David II, King of Scotland, was conveyed in triumph through England to the Tower of London.

The English losses are not known, although in such a fiercely contested battle they must have been severe. The Scots undoubtedly lost the more. It is said that, out of 30,000 men, nearly half perished on the spot and many more in the subsequent pursuit.

And so the year 1346 became a year of victories; the Tower of London did not seem to have sufficient rooms to accommodate all its royal and noble prisoners of war. England was a young nation, only recently united and just finding her feet; the victorious exploits of her soldiers, which had given them a fearsome reputation in an amazingly short space of time, had aroused a spirit of national pride and consciousness never to be lost. By methods derived from his grandfather, Edward III had blended with skill and experience tactical methods that were to be forged in the fires of success at Halidon Hill, Morlaix, Crécy, Neville's Cross and many subsequent victories. To carry out these methods, Edward had at his disposal men of the highest class – men-at-arms who were the pick of the country, and archers who had brought their craft to a peak of perfection by long practice. There are numerous French writings and chronicles that testify to the fearsome and deadly impressions that these archers had made upon continental soldiery. It was indeed a time of national rejoicing that the lusty English infant had learned to walk and was now laying about him so that his presence was to be known through his power of arms for many centuries.

14

Mauron – 1352

So colourful and vital are the victories of Crécy in 1346 and at Poitiers in 1356 that the intervening years of the Hundred Years War tend to assume interest-lacking qualities so far as battles and engagements are concerned. This is due, in part, to the Black Death in 1348 causing so many deaths in England that it became difficult to reinforce the many English garrisons in France, so that there was an inevitable lull in activities. There was also a truce of sorts signed in 1347 which obviously would have prevented major conflicts, for a short time anyway.

In spite of this, it is true to say that throughout this period in question there was almost constant fighting taking place in Picardy, in Brittany and in Gascony. Nor did France cease to try to assuage her pride by recapturing Calais, that festering wound kept open by England for so long. In 1350, there was another naval battle fought off Winchelsea, when fifty small English ships bearing Edward and the cream of his commanders totally defeated – in the best Sluys manner – a Spanish fleet of forty-four much larger and more powerful ships of war. The Queen, with her ladies, sat upon the cliffs looking down at the battle as if it had been a joust or a tourney. It was a sight worth seeing, for all the best in England was out on the water that day – they went forth in little ships and came back in great galleys. Of the tall ships of Spain, more than two score flew the cross of St George before the sun had set.

While it is certain that those land engagements that took pace were fought in the same pattern as those that had preceded them (reminding one of another war between the two countries to be fought some five hundred years later, when circumstances caused the Duke of Wellington to remark that the French continued to attack in column and the British to defeat them in line!), there is evidence that the French were trying to discover the weak points in this frighteningly successful English tactical method. In the summer of 1349, English and Gascon allies, under the Captal de Buch, were involved in a small battle at Lunalonge in Poitou with a French force under Jean de Lisle. By going round to the rear of the position, the French captured the English horses that had been haltered there when the English men-at-arms dismounted as usual and took up battle formations. Having shown such a spark of common sense, the elated French, still mounted, then attacked the English position from the front in the same old manner and were totally defeated, their commander being captured!

In the spring of 1351 a French army under the command of two marshals of France – Guy de Nesle (Sire d'Offrement) and Arnaud d'Endreghem – drove back the weak English garrisons in the province of Poitou and laid siege to Saintes. Seeing that the French king evidently intended to recapture the province, Edward sent Sir John Beauchamp to combat the threat. Beauchamp's army advanced north and the French came to meet them, the two armies approaching each other near St Georges-la-Valade. In their usual manner, the English dismounted and formed line of battle, their horses being sent to the rear under guard of pages. On this occasion the French did the same, but retained two mounted bodies, one on each wing. On foot, like their enemies, the French now attacked frontally and were beaten back, suffering a most decisive defeat and losing 600 men, including the two marshals with 140 esquires and gentlemen. There are no details available of this battle, although it indicates that, in desperation, the French were endeavouring to counter the English tactics by similarly dismounting. Their efforts bore no fruit because they obviously failed to appreciate the full implications of the move.

Marshal de Nesle, having been ransomed after his capture at St Georges-la-Valade, led a French invasion of Brittany in early August 1352, his ultimate objective being Brest. Rennes fell to the French and the English commander, Sir William Bentley, decided to advance northwards towards the Brest road in order to meet the enemy. He decided upon this course of action although he knew himself to be heavily outnumbered, an indication of the confidence with which the English commanders approached the business in hand.

By noon on the 14th of August both armies were approaching the small town of Mauron from different directions; an encounter seemed certain. The dust clouds rising in the north-east indicated to Sir William Bentley that the enemy were approaching. At once his training and experience came into play and he began to seek a position where he could defensively face the enemy in the traditional English dismounted manner. He was fortunate that such a site existed in his vicinity – it was not ideal but good enough to be taken up with reasonable confidence.

The town of Mauron was situated on a ridge, from which a spur ran eastwards with a slope running down to a small rivulet, on the far side of which the ground sloped upwards in gentle fashion, except to the north-east, where it became very steep. The English formed up on the commanding ground of the spur, their centre midway between a narrow belt of trees that ran across the top of the spur and the rivulet; their right rested on a small chateau where the slope was most gentle; there was steeper, almost precipitous, ground near the Rennes road and in front of their left flank. For a force of only about 3,000 men it was a long frontage – nearly 700 yards – and, as at Agincourt in later years, they lacked sufficient men to form a reserve. The country around was open and lacked hedges, ditches or woods; immediately in front of the English position lay a profusion of rank, long undergrowth in full summer flower.

The formation adopted by the English was the one invariably successful in the war – men-at-arms in the centre, and archers in 'herces' or bastions, on the flanks. The centre of the line was about 200 yards from the belt of trees and the flanks curved back slightly towards them, thus conforming to the contours of the ground. This meant that the archers could not cover the whole of the English frontage with their fire.

On the opposite side of the valley, in full view of the English, Guy de Nesle deployed his army; they quite obviously outnumbered the English considerably. He sent across a herald with terms for a withdrawal, terms which were scornfully rejected by Sir William Bentley. So the French carried on dismounting, Nesle evidently retaining confidence in the method that had brought him defeat when last he had met the English, although he retained a mounted body of about 700 men, under command of the Count Hangest, who were to operate on the left wing. This body began the action at four o'clock, when they came into brisk contact with the English archers on the right flank, who immediately gave way and fled! This not only meant that the men-at-arms on their left had no covering fire, but it also exposed their right flank, so they, in their turn, had to fall back up the slope until they reached the belt of trees.

The archers on the left, with no mounted attack to face because of the steeper ground to their front, stood their ground and used their weapons to such good effect that the French men-at-arms did not even reach them but broke and fled under the hail of arrows, scattering pell-mell down the slope. This meant that the right flank of their centre column lay exposed. Then came an example of the great initiative and offensive spirit that hallmarked the English archers throughout the Hundred Years War – the left wing bowmen dropped their bows, drew their swords and charged nimbly down the hill after the retreating French men-at-arms. Some of them swung to the right and attacked the exposed flank of the French centre column, causing disorder and panic.

The English men-at-arms on the right wing, who had formed a defensive line along the edge of the belt of trees, had brought to a partial halt the French horsemen who were pursuing the fleeing archers. Now, encouraged by the English success on the left, they took heart and, fighting fiercely every inch of the way, gradually advanced to push their opponents down the slope before them. Now openly retreating, the French were forced back until they reached the bottom of the valley; as they lumbered laboriously back in the hot summer sun, they were caught in a murderous crossfire of English arrows and suffered heavily. The fleeing French right wing reached the bottom of the valley to find themselves confronted with steep, rearing slopes that formed the only route to safety. Frantically they tried to claw their armoured way up these slopes. Like stricken beetles, their movements became progressively slower until, almost motionless except for feeble movements of their arms, they were shot down unmercifully from short range.

With the exception of Hangest and his cavalry, the French army had dissolved like a piece of ice left in the hot sun. Their leader dead along with most of his senior captains, the rest fled in all directions, intent on saving themselves, leaving more than 2,000 dead on the field.

Yet another victory had been gained by the English archer in the continuous series of contests between himself and the French men-at-arms, a success marred only by the exceptional flight of the right-flank bowmen. The reasons for this flight can only lie in the realms of conjecture – it might have been that Hangest's cavalry were of vastly exceptional quality or, more likely, that the archers themselves were of a lower standard than usual. The huge death roll of the Black Death had meant that the very bottom of the barrel had had to be scraped to reinforce the English armies in France. It must be taken into account that Hangest himself, the French cavalry leader, had shown himself to be a reasonably able commander in the manner in which he had led his men over favourable ground towards the English right flank. By such a move he had prevented more than half the English archers from bringing fire to bear upon his approaching cavalry – this is assuming that they were in the 'herce' formation. Sufficient to say that Bentley had thirty of the archers executed for cowardice on the following day!

As a link between the battles of Crécy and Poitiers, the affair at Mauron forms a very interesting connection in that it confirmed the superiority of the English archer in a frontal attack. It also oddly foreshadowed Poitiers, to a certain extent, in that it contained a mounted flank attack and a downhill counter-attack – both successful in each case.

15

Poitiers – 1356

The Battle of Poitiers (spelt 'Peyters' by the Black Prince) was the second of the great trinity of memorable victories, of which Crécy was the first and Agincourt the third. Although its details are somewhat controversial, it is fair to claim that it is easily the most interesting and instructive of them all from a military point of view. The Black Prince had left Bordeaux on the 6th of July 1356, with the intention of carrying fire and sword into the enemy's domains, endeavouring to meet and destroy the French army in the process and, finally, to join hands somewhere on the line of the river Loire with his uncle, the Duke of Lancaster. But, by early September, the tryst had failed to materialise and the Black Prince had King John of France on his heels with a much larger army than his own. Nevertheless, he sought battle with the French because he correctly reasoned that only by dispersing the numerically superior French army could he get back to Bordeaux with the substantial booty collected during the raid he had made into the heart of France. He was also aware of the high state of his army's morale after ten years of superiority in France; he knew that they had unbounded confidence in him, in fact they held him in holy awe; in return he had no less faith in them.

On the night of Saturday, 17th of September, the French army encamped just outside the walls of Poitiers; the English army lay three miles to the west, in the forest near the little village of Chabotrie. Most of the following day was spent in fruitless discussions between emissaries of the two armies, during a truce period engineered by the Cardinal de Périgord. The terms proposed by King John were too humiliating for the Prince to accept; he fell back on the plea that he was not authorised by his father to so arrange a truce. With nothing concluded, darkness fell and both armies lay on their arms within bowshot of each other. During this night the English held a war council to decide upon a course of action should King John decline indefinitely to attack them. Such a course would inevitably mean that they could be starved into surrender in a few days, whilst the French army steadily increased in size as fresh reinforcements arrived. Prince Edward, although wishing for battle, had seriously to consider the advisability of slipping away, and, in fact, moved the booty-wagons during the night over the Nouaille bridge.

From earliest dawn the camp was alive with the neighing of horses and the clank of armour being donned. In his pavilion, the Black Prince himself was being arrayed for battle; over his head was drawn the shirt of chain mail, reinforced with breast-plate and backplate with shoulder- and arm-guards of burnished steel plates. Next he donned waist-piece and loin-guard, and thigh-pieces, knee-guards, greaves and shoes of jointed mail – the whole an ingeniously fitted combination of chain mail and steel plates. Later, when action was imminent, the great visored helm would be placed over his head, with a coif of flexible mail to protect the neck, and the iron gauntlets would be drawn upon the hands. Piece by piece the jointed plates were fixed to shoulder, elbow, hip, knee and instep, so as to permit of the greatest freedom of movement possible; and all was securely made fast with buckles, locks and rivets. Over all was drawn a jupon or sleeveless tunic of cloth, emblazoned with the heraldic insignia of the Black Prince.

On the morning of the 19th, after the end of the truce at 7.30, the rest of the wagons and their escort bagan to move off. From their vantage point on the North Ridge, the French vanguard spotted the movement and, fearing that the English were going to escape, the two marshals commanding the force decided to attack at once.

The English position had been carefully selected on a ridge facing towards Poitiers; it also covered the road or roads by which the ultimate retirement to Bordeaux would have to be carried out – both these roads are still in existence. There were two ridges, the foremost lying 400 yards to the north-west of Maupertuis, called the North Ridge, the rear one being 400 yards south of it and occupied by the English army for about a thousand yards. It was an uncultivated hill-top, thick with scrub and undergrowth bounded by a hedge, the lower left-hand end of which fell away to a marsh that ran down to join the Moisson river; the upper or right-hand end rested on open ground on top of the plateau and was strengthened by a leaguer made up of the wagons. There were two gaps in the hedge, where the tracks ran through it, the upper gap being left open and the lower barricaded with stakes interlaced with vine branches. Between this ridge and the North Ridge, occupied by the French, lay cultivated land partly vines and partly fallow. At the highest point of the English ridge were two tall trees probably marking the approximate situation of the Black Prince's command post, from where a good view of the whole position and the French line of attack could be obtained. Behind the position the ground sloped up gently for some 500 yards to a large wood, the Nouaille Wood, which in turn dipped down to the valley of the Moisson, 100 feet below.

The English army was about 6,000 strong, composed of 3,000 men-at-arms, 2,000 archers and 1,000 sergeants; the force was positioned along or close to the hedge. Salisbury's division was on the right, Warwick's on the left. The archers, dismounted, were for the most part drawn up in the familiar Crécy formation – on the flanks of their respective divisions, in wedges slightly in advance of the men-at-arms. The Prince's division were in reserve in rear, and he also kept back a small body of mounted men.

The French army was about 20,000 strong, formed in four bodies; in the van were two small contingents of mounted men-at-arms – about 250 each – under the command of the two marshals, Clermont and Audrehem. The leading division was under the command of the Duke of Normandy, the Dauphin; then came that of his uncle, the Duke of Orléans; and, last of all, that of the King, who had given considerable thought to the manner in which his troops were to go into the battle. He had resolved to follow the successful expedient of King Edward at Crécy, and tried by the French without success at St Georges-la-Valade and Mauron. He was going to dismount his men-at-arms, their horses being left in the city of Poitiers. For convenience in marching they had removed their spurs and cut off the long toes of their riding boots; they had also shortened their lances to about five feet for close-quarter fighting.

It was a transitional period so far as armour was concerned; mail was gradually being replaced by plate-armour. The Black Prince wore plate except for his mail gorget, but the ordinary

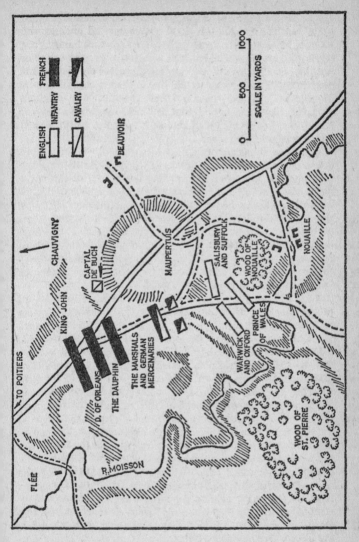

Battle of
Poitiers
*19th
September
1356*

ENGLISH FRENCH
INFANTRY
CAVALRY

TO POITIERS

CHAUVIGNY

KING JOHN

CAPTAL
DE BUCH

D. OF ORLEANS

THE DAUPHIN

THE MARSHALS
AND GERMAN
MERCENARIES

FLÉE

R. MOISSON

MAUPERTUIS

BEAUVOIR

SALISBURY
AND SUFFOLK

WOOD OF
NOUAILLE

NOUAILLE

WARWICK
AND OXFORD

PRINCE
OF WALES

WOOD OF
ST. PIERRE

0   500   1000
SCALE IN YARDS

knight wore a bigger proportion of mail, esquires had even less plate than the knights. Over the breastplate or hauberk was worn a spectacularly emblazoned and loose-fitting surcoat, bearing the arms of the knight who wore it; this gave a recognised rallying point for his followers during any crisis or emergency in the battle. As the strength of armour increased, so the need for the shield diminished – its size decreased until it was eventually discarded. The archers, both foot and mounted, wore a steel cap and breastplate or a padded hauberk. Spearmen were similarly attired, except that they rarely ever wore a breastplate.

Although taking the precaution of sending his booty-wagons off in advance, the Black Prince was inviting battle now that the armistice had ended. The stirring within the French lines as they noted the movement of his transport told the Prince that his gauntlet had been taken up. He passed along the lines of troops, making an inspiring address that subordinate commanders were carefully ordered to pass on to those men who could not actually hear it; then he made a second speech to his archers. His men turned their faces towards the enemy. They were ready for them and confident that victory would be theirs, as it had been at Crécy ten years before.

The two marshals led the small mounted French van forward to the attack by divergent paths, threading their way through the vineyard so that they became a series of small columns each pursuing its own track. Clermont's column tended to bunch leftwards on the Nouaille road, whilst Audrehem followed the Gué de l'Homme track, each path bringing the two columns up against the twin gaps through which the respective tracks breached the hedge. Audrehem's men found themselves facing a manned barricade that held up their advance, so that their leader impatiently thrust himself forward. Being mounted on a better horse than his followers, he succeeded in either jumping or forcing himself through the barricade; unfortunately no one followed him in support so that he was quickly captured and disarmed. Clermont's column came up to the unguarded gap on the Nouaille road; their leading files passed through it and then ponderously swung right to support Audrehem. It was a well-devised manoeuvre that was only frustrated by quick thinking on the part of Salisbury. Immediately weighing up the situation, he moved his line quickly forward right up to the hedge, thus closing the gap and preventing a flank attack on Warwick's division. The fighting that now ensued was severe and some of the cavalry actually managed to break through the centre, but were eventually brought down.

Seeing the approach of the French cavalry, the English archers on the left of the position intelligently moved still further leftwards, into the marsh. In the waterlogged ground they were comparatively safe from the heavily clad horsemen, and, undisturbed, were able to keep up a galling shower of arrows into the French flanks. The move into the marsh took place as a direct result of an order from the Earl of Oxford, who ran down from the Prince's command-post to direct the archers to change their position. He had noticed that the English arrows were ricocheting off the French breastplates as the riders advanced directly towards the archers; the new position enabled them to fire obliquely at the unprotected hindquarters of the horses rather than at the armoured riders.

The slope became littered with dead and wounded men and horses rolling over each other in heaps; one survivor, de Mézerary saying: '. . . the Englishmen's bearded arrows made the horses mad.' Recognising that only the vanguard had been engaged, the English were rigidly restrained from pursuit when the survivors broke and fled.

Now the battle was taken up by the Dauphin's division, who advanced on foot, their shortened but still clumsy lances projecting in front of them as they slowly waddled forward. They were far from happy at what lay before them, their morale having been detrimentally affected by what they had just seen happen to the mounted vanguard. The situation was worsened by the confusion and disorder that rippled through their closely packed ranks as the panic-stricken horses crashed through them in their lumbering passage to the rear, away from the biting arrows that tormented them. It was literally a charge of mad animals, the most terrible of all charges; and it caused the greatest confusion in their ranks.

The English archers fired as quickly as they could, keeping the autumn sky black with their shafts and causing the belaboured French men-at-arms to lurch forward, heads down, falling over the bodies of those who fell before them. Still they came on, moving ever forward in a courageous manner, but courage does not always win battles and it was not to do so in this case. The English fire began to slacken as the archers ran out of arrows; encouraged by this noticeable diminution in the rain of death, the French men-at-arms tramped forward even more resolutely towards the waiting English. As the enemy neared their position, the dismounted English men-at-arms moved forward to the front of the now battered and partly flattened hedge, to give themselves more space to swing their swords in the mêlée that was about to come.

With shouts, battle-cries and the clash of steel, the two forces met and a fierce hand-to-hand struggle took place. It surged back and forth, broke into innumerable personal duels and ebbed to and fro, giving promise of victory first to one side, then the other. Warwick's portion of the line was particularly strained and the Prince reinforced it with the bulk of his own division, keeping a small mounted reserve in hand. At last, with both sides exhausted and hardly able to lift their heavy arms, the Dauphin's men wavered and began to draw off, but still fighting valiantly and in good order.

The hard-breathing English stood back, leaning heavily on their weapons; they were too tired for any spontaneous expressions of triumph but they heaved sighs of relief at what they believed to be the victorious end of the battle. The archers scampered forward to retrieve arrows that they had already discharged and which carpeted the ground in front of them. Water was brought and wounds were dressed, damaged weapons changed for whole ones, a fair selection being possible from those lying around abandoned by dead and wounded of both sides. The English savoured the lengthening lull, taking time to look around them; they failed to realise that there were still two French columns so far uncommitted, at least one of which was double the strength of the entire English army. This impression was so marked that a number of men-at-arms were actually sent off in pursuit of the Dauphin's retreating men.

The original plan of the King of France was for the next stage of the battle to be taken up by the column of the young Duke of Orléans; but it had completely dispersed and was fleeing in scattered groups towards Chauvigny. The disastrous effects of the two distinct and separate groups of survivors from previous attacks fleeing, weaponless and distraught, through their ranks, caused a panic that their twenty-one-year-old commander was completely unable to stem.

For some reason the King's column was being held far back behind the fighting, so that the Dauphin's force had been dispersed before John even knew that they had been engaged. He was now aware that only his 10,000 men remained, and he had ominous doubts as to whether they could cope with even the 6,000 or so battle-weary English who remained secure in their position on the ridge. The most prudent move would have been a strategical withdrawal but there were considerations of chivalry to be taken into account and, as a typical example of French thinking of the day, high-minded dreams prevailed over discretion. King John gave the order to advance; slowly, stiffly the column rolled forward to the attack, lumbering arduously to the top of the North Ridge facing the English position.

The serried ranks of the large, glittering mass topped the ridge in good order, banners fluttering, weapons gleaming; apparently unaffected by what had gone before, they moved purposefully to the attack. When the formidable spectacle was unrolled before their eyes, the weary English gaped in astonishment; their previous elation suddenly disappeared and was replaced by exhaustion and apprehension. Dismayed curses and grumbles rose on all sides. Many looked wildly around as though seeking an avenue of escape; losing his head, one of the Prince's staff cried out:

'Alas! We are beaten!'

His master looked at him contemptuously and then turned away. Raising his head so that all around him could hear, the Prince stingingly replied:

'Thou liest! Thou knave! If thou sayest that we can be conquered as long as I live!'

Nevertheless, it was a decisive moment in the life of the Black Prince. He did not know of the defection of the Duke of Orléans' column and was uncertain whether or not it was backing up this great, fresh force that was steadily lumbering towards them. He had to make a rapid decision; should he sacrifice some of his foot soldiers and the wagons, be satisfied with the damage he had done up to now, and withdraw? Or should he repeat the action that had already taken place twice and stand on the defensive and let them throw themselves against his tired men? No, he did not fancy that, realising that, for the moment, his moral superiority had departed and he recalled a tactical point that he had earlier noticed – that his defensive position was less effective against dismounted men than against cavalry.

The Prince's active brain seized on the one and only course that would restore his army's morale – he would attack! He reasoned swiftly to himself – the French were out in the open, on the move and dismounted, and they lacked archers – all factors that added up to a marked inability to defend themselves against a mounted attack. The Prince blessed the inspiration that had caused him to keep his horses at hand and order spurs to be retained by his men-at-arms. If the Prince had any doubts about his plan, they were rapidly dispersed when Sir John Chandos, one of his ablest commanders, hastened to his side and urgently spoke:

'Sir, ride forward, the days is yours! Let us assail the King of France, for with him lies all the strength of the enterprise. Well I know his valour will not permit him to flee, therefore, please God and Saint George, he shall remain with us!'

On all sides, commanders roared out orders to mount; the men-at-arms, their previous exhaustion forgotten in the new excitement, gathered themselves together and struggled into the saddle, where they slumped awaiting the next order. Becoming impatient through the delay that followed, their horses restlessly lifted their feet and nudged into each other, whilst their riders glanced to both sides seeking the reason for the pause. The Prince was arranging a diversion in the form of a flank attack by the small mounted reserve he still held, fresh and ready, under the Gascon leader, Captal de Buch. He carefully instructed them to leave the position by the northern end of the Nouaille wood, swing left and approach the North Ridge unobserved, so that they hit the French left flank as their column trudged forward. The Prince returned to the head of his men, glanced all around him, nodded with satisfaction and raised his sword high above his head. To the standard-bearers he cried:

'Advance, banners! In the name of God and St George!'

With the Prince and Chandos in front, the now mounted men-at-arms rolled down the slope towards the dip that lay between them and the North Ridge, gradually gathering momentum as they went. Having exhausted their arrows, the mounted archers drew their swords and grimly tacked themselves on to the flanks and rear of the now charging mass. The advancing French division, seeing the sudden avalanche of men and horses cascading down towards them, backed by the thunder of hooves and the shouts of battle-cries, involuntarily stopped, so that the rear ranks piled up on those in front. For some it proved too much; a considerable number of the French men-at-arms in the rear and on the flanks took advantage of their position to turn and run, shambling from the field as fast as their heavy armour allowed. Before the remainder could assume any sort of defensive position or formation, change their ranks or present a more united front, the English horsemen were upon them. They crashed home into the wall of yielding, living bodies with a fierce shock that tumbled men of both sides, together with horses, to the ground.

Now ensued a hard and bloody conflict; the mounted English

were still outnumbered but managed to force their way forward yard by yard. It was the closest of close-quarter fighting where the short dagger was more deadly than the five-foot lance that could not be plunged home, or the sword that lacked space in which to be wielded.

This was the time when conflict sounded and looked possibly more deadly than it actually was, if one is only to consider those men-at-arms actually killed by opposing men-at-arms. In those cases the actual killing was seldom great but many were unhorsed or thrown to the ground, where they lay helpless until assisted to rise again; in hot weather many were suffocated or choked in blood if their visors were not unclasped. Those among them who perished by sword-cut or lance-thrust were few in comparison to the slaughter made when they found an opening in a formation of infantry, or came upon unsupported archers without having to take too many arrows.

The mêlèe surged back and forth, the ground became slippery and bloody, men tumbled noisily, to be trampled into shapeless hulks beneath the shuffling feet and hooves of the combatants; on all sides the air was full of the tumult of battle.

Under such conditions it was not surprising that no one saw the approach of Captal de Buch's small body of cavalry as they came in on the French left flank. They crashed into this unsuspecting part of the King's division with a shock result, both physically and morally, far in excess of their size and numbers. Resolutely they commenced to hack their way into the mêlée. For the French it was the last straw; their great column, attacked on two sides, began to crumble like a sandcastle under the onslaught of remorseless waves. Progressively, it slowly disintegrated as men stole, stumbled and lurched from the field, seeking safety and wildly gazing in every direction for sanctuary. The more faithful followers of the King of France fought bravely around him; the Black Prince and his commanders kept their men steadily on hand, concentrating their efforts on this confused multitude who still fought on, being whittled down by sword, axe, lance and dagger. The King himself fought bravely, battle-axe in hands almost too weary to wield it; around him pressed a furious throng of English and Gascons, crying:

'Surrender! Give way!'

Anxious to save the French monarch, many English knights implored him to yield but he was unwilling to do so to anyone of inferior rank. Repeatedly he asked:

'Where is my cousin? Where is the Prince of Wales?'

A young knight of St Omer spoke to him in French:

'Sire, surrender! I will lead you to him.'

Struck by his pure accent, the breathless, weary King asked:
'Who are you?'

'Sire, I am Denis of Norbeque, a knight of Artois. I serve the King of England because I have lost my all in France.'

The King sighed:

'Then, to you I surrender.'

He gave the young knight his right gauntlet and moved slowly with him towards the edge of the mêlée, where some Gascons and English claimed him and tried to wrest him away from Norbeque. The opportune arrival of the Earl of Warwick and Sir John Pelham saved what might well have been a disastrous ending. The English knights approached the royal captive with every show of respect and conducted him to the Prince of Wales.

Slowly the battle burned itself out; the triumphant English pursued some of the fleeing French as far as the very walls of Poitiers. Amid the dead and dying, the Black Prince had his pavilion pitched and there, with darkness descending, sat down to dine with his royal prisoner of war.

The French casualties amounted to approximately 2,500 reported killed and some 2,000 captured, plus about 4,000 wounded; no record seems to have been kept of the casualties to the infantry levies, whose battered bodies were piled into a great charnel-pit. Although no accurate figures are available, apparently the English got off very lightly.

There were a number of valid reasons for the English victory at Poitiers; a success prominent among the consistent English victories over numerically stronger forces that marked this sixteen-year period in the middle of the fourteenth century. In a way, Poitiers was a throw-back to the previous century in that it was won by men-at-arms with a successful late action of mounted against dismounted troops. Although it began in the Crécy tradition, the archers did not really play their usual prominent part.

The eventual result of the battle was much affected by the manner in which the two opposing commanders handled their armies. The Black Prince never let go his strong personal grip; he most adequately utilised the lull after beating off the Dauphin's attack by brilliantly deciding to mount and attack, coupling the onslaught with a mounted flank attack. He chose his ground well in that it was suitable for the size of his army; the hedge served its purpose admirably, the vineyard in front broke up the cavalry attacks, and the nature of the ground on the right lent itself to the flank move. The Prince gave his force mobility by keeping his horses handy – without this there could have been no combined frontal and flank attack, so unusual for battles of the period.

On the other hand, King John of France lacked combined control over his forces, who were formed into what amounted to three distinct and separate armies. This is reflected in the manner in which he allowed his own division to be so far behind the battlefield at the time when the Dauphin was being repulsed; at that moment he should have been handy and ready to take it up again. Instead his men had a long and slow advance to make, giving the Black Prince time to formulate alternative, winning tactics. Obsessed with King Edward's defence at Crécy, King John dismounted his men-at-arms, but failed to observe that the circumstances were absolutely different in that he required a vigorous impact through shock and mobility, whereas Edward sought defensive stability. Coupled with this error and connected with his lack of overall control, the French King allowed his army to be formed into one gigantic wedge that, division by division, dashed itself against the strongest part of the English position.

So ended another French king's attempt to defeat the English army in France, a failure attended by even greater ignominy than that of his predecessor at Crécy.

16

Homildon Hill – 1402

The royal captive from Poitiers was marched in triumph through London and, eventually, a two years' truce was signed. Sought as a healing-time, this period became one of internal warfare between bands of routed soldiery who formed themselves into free companies of bandits; the miserable country that was France found no rest in herself. Next, Paris rose against the Crown in a rising that was hardly crushed before Edward was again ravaging the wasted land. The defeat at Poitiers had such a profound effect upon the French military mind that they made no further attempts to meet the English in a pitched land battle. They allowed the English to wear themselves out marching the length and breadth of the land, whilst they sullenly shut themselves in their castles. Famine was proving France's best defence, so that these tactics were reasonably well suited to the circumstances; but they inevitably drove yet another nail into the coffin of chivalry by being opposed to every precept of that feudal state which bade every good knight to accept each and all challenges.

At last both countries seemed to be worn out. Edward's army had fallen back on the Loire when proposals of peace reached them. By the Treaty of Bretigny, in May 1360, Edward waived his claims on the crown of France and on the Duchy of Normandy; on the other hand, the Duchy of Aquitaine, which included Gascony, Guienne, Poitou, Saintonge, Limousin, Périgord and Rouergue, were left to him, no longer as a fief but in full sovereignty, while his new conquest of Calais remained a part of the possessions of the English crown. Edward also retained the country of Ponthieu (with Abbeville and the site of Crécy) on the Channel Coast. If it was not all that Edward wanted, it was still triumph; a triumph well earned by the dominant monarch whose personality and persistence had brought victory. Possessing a natural talent for war, his attitude and methods inspired confidence in the rugged, experienced and gifted commanders he had gathered around himself. It was a confidence that flowed naturally from them down to the rank-and-file, leading to a vibrant morale and a high level of discipline. When the Treaty of Bretigny was signed, there was little doubt that the English soldier and, therefore, the English army formed a professional body of fighting men without equal in the world. Only in this way was it able so consistently to defeat one several times larger than itself, its campaigning bringing a polished experience that refused to accept the existence of anything less than overwhelming victory.

England was a young nation and its fires of national consciousness were to be stoked up by this series of Continental successes, bringing with them a pride that has never left these shores. It is probably no mere coincidence that the signing of the Treaty of Bretigny practically coincided with the introduction of the English tongue into Parliamentary proceedings. The incontestable military superiority of the English in the fourteenth century lay, above all, in the dexterity with which they used good weapons combined with the high proportion of archers to other arms. With this must be coupled the high standards of English morale; they entered the Hundred Years War with a reasonably high state of morale, due to the successes against the Scots; by Poitiers this mental state was at its very peak among both officers and men.

Although a treaty had been signed, the men who fought still had ability and hot blood to put at the disposal of anyone who needed first-class fighting men and could pay well for them. On the 16th of March 1364 a Free Company of English archers, numbering about 300, fought for the King of Navarre against the King of France at Cockerel. It was a small battle, only about 1,500 on each side, but made notable by attempts of the French to combat the now familiar English tactics. They dismounted their men-at-arms, who fought on foot, their armour being of such superior quality that it turned the English arrows. Coupled with a slight superiority in numbers, this factor forced the King of Navarre's men from the field. It was only a very slight success, but the defeat of even a small body of English was such a rarity in those days that it aroused great hopes in French breasts for the future.

The following year saw a battle at Auray, on the 29th of September, 1365 when English troops aided John of Montfort in his quarrel with Charles of Blois. The forces were small again, about 4,000 a side; both dismounted and the French discarded their lances, to fight with battle-axe and sword. The English archers opened the engagement, but, as at Cockerel, their shafts could not penetrate the French armour. After some futile shooting, with great deliberation, they threw down their bows and boldly advanced towards the French men-at-arms. Their lightness of foot and nimble tactics are said to have enabled them literally to 'run rings around' the armoured men, whose axes and swords they plucked from their hands and used against their former owners! In a series of detached struggles between brawny, active Englishmen in doublet and hose against panting Frenchmen cased stiffly in mail and plate-armour, staggering and rattling as they cursed from behind closed visors, the struggle swayed back and forth. Quickly, men-at-arms came to the assistance of the archers, and, after a desperate engagement, the French were driven from the field of battle.

In the year 1377 the French landed a considerable body of troops on the Isle of Wight; they took and razed the city of

Francheville,[1] and then, splitting into two columns, made for the fortress of Carisbrooke. The first column, ambushed by English archers, was completely wiped out; the second was so sorely beaten, again by bowmen, at the castle, that the French were forced to retreat. At this time Richard II was King of England; records indicate that he maintained a standing body-guard of archers, some authorities placing their numbers as high as 4,000. On one occasion, when trouble arose in London, the bodyguard, fearing for the life of their master, drew their arrows and ranked themselves outside Parliament, it is said, 'to the terror of the people.'

Towards the end of the fourteenth century the armour of the period became much more elaborate, partaking of the more extravagant modes of the age. Plate was so universally worn that the gussets of chain at the joints and the chain apron were all that remained of the old mail of the tenth century. The jupon and military girdle were still worn, and visored bascinets were some-times used, with the ventaille fashioned like the beak of a bird, while the bascinet itself was often encircled by a band or fillet of ermine, or a border of beautiful workmanship, Milan was now the grand emporium for equipping the chivalry of Europe. Heraldic crests on the helmet were worn in England by all men of rank, but not generally used in Scotland for almost a hundred years after being common in England. The armour of the Earl of Douglas, defeated Scots commander at Homildon Hill, was said to have taken a year to temper and make.

The old enemy, the Scots, ever on the lookout for an oppor-tunity to profit by England's occupation in other directions, crossed the border in September 1402, and penetrated as far as Newcastle. Under the leadership of Archibald, fourth Earl of Douglas, the Scots force, numbering perhaps 8,000, laid waste the land and then turned back towards the border. Henry IV being engaged at the time on a Welsh expedition, an English force to oppose the Scots was hastily collected under the leader-ship of the Earl of Northumberland and his son, the gallant Hotspur. These experienced border leaders, together with the Earl of March, decided to intercept the Scots when on their homeward march, encumbered with spoil and herds of cattle.

1. The Borough of Francheville is now known as *Newtown*, Isle of Wight. It is now a minute, decayed village but was once a populous and thriving town with a harbour. In its day it was superior in size and commercial prosperity to neighbouring Newport. It was sacked and burned many times during its early existence.

The Earl of Douglas was at Wooler when he received the news that his way to Scotland was barred by an English force at Millfield, on the river Till, about five miles north-west of Wooler. Douglas immediately took up a position on an eminence, Homildon Hill, about two miles west by north of Wooler. The hill itself was terraced in three successive tiers, and had an elevation of nearly 1,000 feet above sea-level; it had a flat top and traces of a rude earthwork were detectable; on its lower slopes burial mounds existed.

Here the Scots were noisily forming themselves into their schiltrons – the defensive formations of pikemen that had served them well in the past – when they were suddenly attacked by a body of about 500 English archers who had been sent forward on a reconnaissance. The bowmen opened fire at long range on their hereditary enemies and caused some damage among the massed Scots ranks; then they came closer and men began to fall fast – well might the archers of England boast that each carried twelve Scots lives at his belt! With Douglas was a small body of archers, who attempted to reply to the hail of English arrows without doing much damage; a fact that can be put down to the Scottish bow being smaller and weaker than its English counterpart, only being pulled to the chest it had a much shorter range. Spasmodically, bodies of Scots spearmen attempted to charge down the hill, but all were thrown back by showers of arrows. Under the galling hail, the national temperament of the fiery Scots rose to boiling point; they began to move from their defensive position and to surge down the hill.

When the surge became a flood, the English archers commenced to retire in sections, discharging volleys in succession, causing the baffled spearmen to lose men at every step as they impulsively pressed forward. A body of Scots horse lumbered to the front but, in the same way, were unable to get into close quarters. It was maddening and ridiculous that this small body of men should be causing such heavy casualties without losing a single man of their own.

The chase, or luring, went on, until the English archers had drawn the entire Scottish force down from their hill to a field known as Red Rigg on the other side of the river Till. Here, the remainder of the English force waited, impatient for action; in fact, Hotspur proposed an immediate charge on the disordered Scots but the Earl of March seized his bridle and suggested that the archers should first be allowed to discharge all their shafts. The Scots attempted to re-form their normally close-packed ranks

115

into a defensive formation when they saw the massed ranks of the English awaiting them, but were still being ruthlessly assailed by the hissing clothyard shafts of the archers. These Scottish pikemen, if they had any armour at all it was only the very lightest, so unprotected and in close-knit groups, fell in dozens upon each other. Their leaders, who still used the old English chain mail, found it no defence against the deadly arrows; horses, wounded and ungovernable, their breasts and flanks bristling with bloody arrows, galloped madly to and fro, trampling both dead and wounded into a gory pulp.

Sir John Swinton, an old Scots knight of distinguished record, cried out bitterly:

'Why stand we thus to be shot down like deer? Where is our wonted courage? Are we to be still as if our hands were nailed to our lances? Follow me and let us at least sell our lives as dearly as we can!'

At the head of about 100 men, he desperately charged forward, completely unsupported by the rest of the Scots army, to be quickly overthrown and destroyed almost to a man. Then Douglas made a final effort to save the day by making a desperate charge at the head of his men. Before the attack broke down under the fire of the archers, Douglas himself had lost an eye and been wounded in four places. When this onslaught came forward, the archers retired before it, dropping back on to their cavalry, but continued to shoot until the advancing Scots wavered and broke.

Percy and March now saw that the time had come to act; they sent in the English mounted men. With a shout, the archers dropped their bows and took to their swords and axes, rushing in and mingling with the horsemen, to play their final part in the mêlée. There was not a great deal for the men-at-arms to do. They drew their swords and laid their lances in rest, but the Scots had had enough; broken by the archers, they turned to flee. They were pursued as far as Coldstream, the old crossing place of the Tweed; it was said by the chroniclers that the Scots' losses in the pursuit were even greater than those of the battle!

In 1403, at the Battle of Shrewsbury, the English had a taste of the fearsome medicine dealt out for so long to the French and the Scots. Positioned on a slope, the Cheshire archers of the rebel Hotspur, filled the air with a deadly hail of arrows, taking heavy toll of Henry IV's men. This first discharge of arrows, was by all accounts, terrifying; Walsingham, a contemporary writer, says: 'They fell upon the King's troops like leaves upon the ground in autumn. Every one struck a mortal man.' Henry V, then the fifteen-year-old Prince Henry, carried to his grave the scar of a facial wound caused by an arrow – he refused to leave the field of combat.

Had the Cheshire archers been able to maintain their shower of shafts the royal army would have been swept from the field. When it slackened, the archers were overcome by the superior numbers of the King's men sweeping up the slope. Within three hours, 1,600 out of 8,000 men had been killed, the majority from arrow wounds.

17

Agincourt – 1415

Taking advantage of the civil war which convulsed France, these internal calamities offering a tempting opportunity for aggression, Henry V, on his accession, revived Edward III's claim to the throne of France. Henry's war was a renewal of the earlier struggle on the expiration of a truce made by Richard. In mid-1415, Henry sailed with his army from Southampton, and in five weeks had reduced the strong fortress of Harfleur. Dysentry and similar diseases made havoc in his ranks during the siege and it was with a mere handful of men that Henry decided to insult the enemy with a daring march, like that of Edward, upon Calais.

On the 8th of October the English marched off in three columns, with cavalry on their flanks. But Henry found the bridges of the river Somme broken down and the fords rendered perilous by lines of pointed stakes in the river bed. After some delay, an undefended place was discovered near St Quentin; he crossed rapidly and marched for Calais, only for his weary, sick and half-starved force to find a much larger French force camped right across their line of march. The English King knew that he had no choice between fighting and unconditional surrender; his troops were starving and the way to Calais lay through the French army. The King's courage rose as his peril grew and, hungry, sick and weary as they were, the handful of men whom he led shared the spirit of their leader.

Amid the darkness of the October night and through the sheets of biting, cold rain, the English could see the whole landscape flickering with the French camp-fires. Over the half-mile of sodden, muddy ground that lay between the armies, the passing wind carried the noise of shouting, singing and bursts of merriment. It contrasted oddly with the disciplined quiet of the English camp, where well-trained soldiers saw to their weapons, confessed and were shriven, chastened by the conviction that most of them would die on the morrow. King Henry took little rest; he moved quietly among his men, talking to them. Once, when a brief season of moonlight occurred, he sent officers out to examine the ground over which they would soon fight.

At three o'clock the moon rose, and the whole army awoke and prepared for the day's work. To keep their hearts cheerful, the King ordered the trumpets, drums and fifes to play familiar tunes. The night passed away and the dawn stole on – the dawn of the Feast of St Crispin, the 25th of October 1415. It had stopped raining but the sky was grey and water-laden; the men began to be deployed by their marshals into order of battle. If they did not present a tidy, colourful appearance, their tarnished, dented and well-used armour and equipment gave them a workman like status that held a hint of what was to come. It had been bright and burnished when they had left Southampton two months before; bright plumes in the apex of the helmet had long since bedraggled and drooped, but the form of the helm itself was still quite beautiful, with an orle or chaplet around it. The breastplates had become globular in recent years and the steel gorget was replacing the ancient camail which had hitherto protected the throat. Hanging sleeves of rich cloth had been worn with the armour, now hanging in threads and tatters. The lance-rests were hooks just below the right breasts; two-handed swords with heavy blades had just been introduced and a pole-axe was often carried by commanders in the field. Monstrelet, in his Chronicles, describes the English archers as being for the most part without armour, and in jackets with their hose loose, without hats or caps and often barefooted; their hatchets or swords hung at their girdle. St Remy says that they were not bareheaded, and that many of them wore caps of *cuir bouilli*, or boiled leather, and others of wicker-work crossed over with bars of iron.

The King heard three Masses, held at various parts of the camp so that all could take part; he was clad in all his armour save his helm and emblazoned surcoat. After the last Mass they brought them to him – the helm was a bascinet with a bavière, upon which he had a crown of gold studded with pearls, sapphires and rubies; his surcoat was resplendent with the leopards of England and the fleur-de-lys of France. He mounted his grey palfrey and rode down the lines of troops, calling out words of encouragement to them as he received their cheers. He spoke to his archers, reminding them that when Soissons had fallen a few months before, the French had hung up like dogs the 300 English archers of the garrison. The common soldier knew that, in defeat, he would be cut down to the last man; not for him was there a life-saving ransom as in the case of the knights.

As he proceeded, Henry chanced to hear someone wish that '. . . some of the good knights who were idle in England might, by a miracle, be transported to this field of battle.'

Henry cried loudly:

'No! I would not have a single man more! If God gives us victory, it will be plain that we owe it to His goodness. If He do not, the fewer we are will be the less loss to England. But fight with your usual courage and God and the justice of our cause shall protect us!'

Another heartening example of spirit and courage was shown by David Gam, a Welsh captain, returning from reconnoitring the enemy, who reported that '. . . there are enough to be killed, enough to be taken and enough to run away!'

The small English army was drawn up on the old plan of Crécy, in the usual three 'battles' of dismounted men-at-arms with archers on the wings of each battle, and a further two bodies of archers, one on each wing of the army. The men-at-arms were about four deep and the archers about seven to the yard, being formed into wedges or bastion-like formations projecting in front of the line of men-at-arms. The centre was commanded by the King, the right wing by Edward, Duke of York, and Lord Camoys commanded the left wing. The total English strength was under 6,000, composed of about 1,000 men-at-arms and knights, with 5,000 archers – a force so small that the King could afford no reserve and only the smallest baggage-guard.

The French army, mainly composed of men-at-arms, was formed in three lines, all being dismounted except the rear one; there were two bodies of cavalry each 600 strong, stationed on each wing. The lines were about five or six deep, although the French front of about 1,200 yards was most congested for their force of about 25,000 men, so that they were densely packed with little space to ply weapons.

The two armies formed up at dawn on that autumn morning

and, for four hours, stood motionless watching each other intently; the French had too many bitter memories of Crécy, Poitiers and other battles to take the offensive, so they stood firm awaiting an English advance. It was an anticlimax that was encouraging to the smaller English force, although very wearing on the nerves!

On the march to Agincourt, Henry had been informed that the French intended to make a 'dead-set' at the hated archers. To combat this, he ordered each archer to provide himself with a stake six feet in length and pointed at each end. In case of mounted attack, or when in position as on this very morning, the stakes were to be thrust into the ground, the upper ends sloping towards the enemy. The chronicler, Holinshed, writing on this, says: 'The King ordered his battle thus: he caused stakes bound with iron sharpe at both ends of the length of five or six foot to be pitched before the archers and on each side of the footmen like a hedge, to the intent that if barded (i.e. armoured) horses run rashlie upon them they might shortlie be gored and destroyed. Certain persons were also appointed to remove the stakes as, by the movement of the archers, occasion and time should require, so that the footmen were hedged about with stakes. This device of fortyfieing the army was at this time first invented.'

During their long wait the men had the chance to view the arena; they saw that they filled one side of a rectangle, the other three sides being formed by the massed French army in front of them; by the Agincourt woods on their left and the Tramcourt woods on their right. The whole was about 940 yards wide at its narrowest point and the two armies were about 1,000 yards apart, with a slight dip between them so that they were in full view of each other. The ground beneath their feet was ploughed, a newly sown wheatfield made very soft and muddy by the tramping of feet after days of heavy rain. Some accounts of the battle claim that Henry had stationed a mounted force of about 400 lances in the Tramcourt woods on the French left, and 200 archers on their right in the Agincourt woods – this seems unlikely in view of his sparse numbers.

Shrewd tactician Henry realised that his only possible chance of victory lay in provoking the much larger French army to attack him; so at eleven o'clock, he ordered his little army to advance to within long-archery range. The cry rang through the still air:

'Advance, banner!'

Everyone knelt down, made a cross upon the ground and

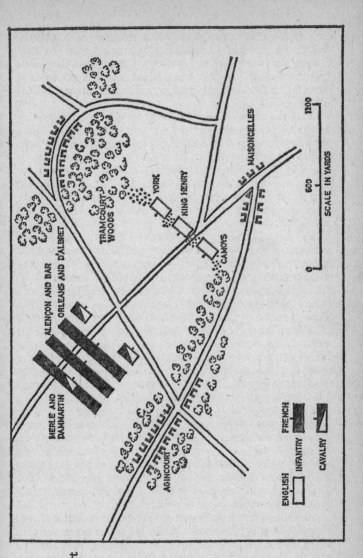

Battle of Agincourt

25th October 1415

ALENÇON AND BAR
ORLEANS AND D'ALBRET

MERLE AND DAMMARTIN

TRAMCOURT WOODS

YORK
KING HENRY
CAMOYS

AGINCOURT

MAISONCELLES

ENGLISH
FRENCH
INFANTRY
CAVALRY

SCALE IN YARDS
0   600   1200

kissed it. Sir Thomas Erpingham, the commander of the archers, repeated the order and his lightly clad men struggled to pluck from the heavy ground the pointed wooden stakes that each had driven before him. Then the whole force slowly began to advance in line, halting occasionally to allow the heavily armoured men-at-arms to regain their breath. When ordered, the archers again planted their stakes in front of them, obliquely pointing towards the French like *chevaux-de-frise;* raising their bows, they opened fire in an attempt to sting the French into advancing. As they fired their first volley the archers raised a loud shout, partly of defiance and partly of sheer pleasure at the prospect of action. The standing about had caused them to chill and stiffen. Many of them had stripped to the waist for freedom of action, but many were naked from the waist down in order to cope with the dysentery from which most of them were suffering.

The French were unable to reply to the fire that quickly became a galling, damaging hail; they had brought with them a small body of crossbowmen but they had been pushed to the rear and could not get forward where they were needed. It was a position they were probably not sorry to be occupying, recalling the story of how the crossbowmen had been trampled down by their own knights at Crécy. At last the French cavalry on the wings began to move forward, the horses obviously stiff and weary from so long standing, the treacherous, muddy ground combined with the weight of their armoured riders causing them to stagger and stumble. At the same moment, the dismounted men-at-arms of the front line began to lurch forward, heavily, across the waterlogged ground, sinking to their ankles in the mud, all the time taking heavy punishment from the English arrows.

The mailed cavalry came nearer to the English lines, floundering through the wet, clayey soil and beset by hails of arrows that took greater toll as the range became shorter. So accurate was the aim of the English archers that most of the arrows struck the knights on their helmets and visors so that many fell shot through the brain; chroniclers report that so terrible was the rain of arrows that all had to bend their heads so as to save their faces. Other archers shot at the horses, killing some but wounding more, making them swerve, halt, plunge and cavort in all directions to cause confusion in the French ranks. So fierce was the fire coming towards them from front and flank that, on the Agincourt woods side, the cavalry led by Sir William de Savense pulled up and turned back, leaving Sir William and only two faithful followers to reach the English position. Here, because of the soft ground, some of the archers' stakes became uprooted, but others caused the horses to fall so that the three riders were thrown heavily to the ground among the archers, to be instantly killed by sword and dagger.

The retreating cavalry, amongst whom were many riderless and unmanageable horses, caused great disorder among the advancing men-at-arms, whose plodding progress was further disorganised by their being crowded in on each other owing to the 'funnelling' of the woods as they came nearer to the English lines. This was further aggravated by the dismounted men, goaded by the showers of arrows, tending to flinch away from the wedges of bowmen towards the three divisions of men-at-arms; this caused further loss of space. Even so, the English line was shaken by the first impact of the heavily armoured formations and a wild, mingled mass of desperately fighting men of all arms filled the area. The archers, dropping their bows, seized their swords and axes and flung themselves into the places where gaps or breaches had been made by the French. The enemy men-at-arms, almost completely exhausted by their struggle through the mud and the subsequent fighting, were no match for their lighter opponents; almost helplessly they stood until beaten to the ground by repeated blows from the archers' weapons. In a short time the French line was thrown back, reeling upon their second 'battle' as they, in their turn, heavily plodded up to join the action. It is not hard to imagine that the archers, a pretty rough lot at the best of times but now with their blood fired by the success of their shooting, were highly effective as they smashed at the struggling, weighted-down men-at-arms with swords, axes, clubs and mauls; or judiciously inserted a sharp dagger into a joint in the armour of a helpless, fallen man.

The English reformed their line and stepped forward to meet the new threat – led by the King, dismounted and fighting on foot, made conspicuous not only by his valour but by his glittering armour, emblazoned surcoat and gleaming crown on his helm. By now a wall of dead and dying had begun to form across the narrow gap between the two woods. It was a wall that was constantly added to by the casualties from the French second line; as it rose higher and higher it was scaled by the agile and lightly armed archers in their efforts to reach the enemy. Some of the frightful piles of dead men reached as high as a man, both sides fighting around them as though they were masonry ramparts. Henry drove back the Duc d'Alençon, who had beaten the Duke of Gloucester to the ground with his battle-axe; in doing so he received a blow that clipped off a portion of the crown on his helm.

D'Alençon and a number of other knights had sworn to kill the King – this they tried desperately to do and the fighting around Henry was deadly and without quarter; finally the dedicated French knights were all killed or lay wounded and helpless.

On all sides the French were being rapidly despatched and the battle was gradually petering out as fewer and fewer Frenchmen remained alive. For them it had been a nightmare. Pressing forward determinedly into the fight, they found it impossible to obtain sufficient room to wield their weapons; a man would be brought crashing to the muddy ground, taking with him those on either side of him, for all to wallow helplessly until despatched by the long, keen daggers of the archers. Defensive armour had become so heavy that there was no getting up once a man was down; in fact, the weighty men falling upon each other frequently caused death by suffocation. This happened to the Duke of York at Agincourt; when his body was found and pulled from the shambles he was unwounded but dead.

Still fresh and in good order and so far uncommitted, the French third line might well have restored the failing fortunes of the day. But they stood, in indecision and dismay, realising that to advance was fruitless and not knowing what else to do, whilst on all sides the faint-hearted slipped away in the confusion. Whilst they stood irresolute, a herald arrived from Henry with a message that they were to leave the field instantly, or receive no quarter; soon they began to melt away.

The two hours that followed were filled with the task of securing prisoners, disentangling the living from the dead, marshalling those who could walk and removing the armour of the wounded and the captives. In the midst of this industry, word flew from mouth to mouth that the enemy had got into the baggage-camp at Maisoncelles! This meant that the French were in the English rear, at present busy pillaging the camp after dispersing the small baggage-guard; at the same time, the French third line reappeared menacingly on the outskirts of the field! The Duke of Brabant had joined their leaders in entreating, threatening and urging them to return to the battle and had been partly successful in that the force had slowly, reluctantly, begun to edge back towards the English; they formed a force that, by itself, outnumbered the whole English army.

Absorbed in their work of collecting prisoners and booty, the English were taken completely off their guard. If they left the prisoners, many of whom were still in their armour, to go and repel the new threat, then the prisoners could pick up weapons and join with the plunderers to attack them in their rear. There seemed little alternative; relucantly Henry ordered all prisoners to be put to the sword; after some murmurings at good ransoms going to waste, the murderous work began and a wholesale massacre took place. When it was seen that the threat of attack had died away with the disappearance of the remaining French troops, the throat-cutting ceased. Froissart, speaking on the Battle of Aljubarrota, where as at Agincourt the handful of victors were obliged by a sudden panic to slay their prisoners, says: 'Lo, behold the great evil adventure that fell that Saturday. For they slew as many good prisoners as would well have been worth, one with another, 400,000 franks.'

The main feature of the battle was the extraordinary numbers of French dead, reports indicating that the numbers reached 10,000. Included among the casualties were half the nobility of France – the Constable of France and Commander-in-Chief, Charles d'Albret, the Dukes of Alençon, Brabant and Bar, the Counts of Nevers, Vaudemont, Marle, Roussi and Falconberg. Among the prisoners were the Dukes of Orléans and Bourbon, Count Arthur of Richmont and Marshal Boucicaut – a clean sweep was made of the highest commanders of France. The English lost the Duke of York, the young Earl of Suffolk and about 1,500 men killed and wounded.

King Henry sent for Mountjoy, a French herald who came for permission to bury the dead. He said to him:

'To whom belongs this victory?'

'To you, sire.'

'And what castle is that which we can perceive in the distance?'

'It is called the castle of Agincourt, sire.'

'Then let this be called the Battle of Agincourt,' said Henry.

18

Verneuil – 1424; and Rouvray – 1428

The immediate result of the Battle of Agincourt was small, for the English army was too exhausted to pursue; it made its way to Calais only to return to England. For a while the war was limited to a contest for the command of the Channel by such sea battles as took place at Harfleur on the 15th of August 1416, the year following Agincourt.

John, Duke of Bedford, commanded a fleet of about 100 ships which dropped anchor in the mouth of the Seine estuary, within sight of the numerically larger fleet of the French. About 150 in number and with some very large vessels among them, they were anchored in midstream. Drawn up in close order in the centre of the estuary between Honfleur and Harfleur, they formed a serried mass with little water-space between each ship. Although he planned to attack, Bedford intended using his archers to gain victory just as they did on land – by driving hostile missile-throwers from shrouds and bulwarks so that the English men-at-arms could board and come to close quarters. The English ships set their sails fully and drove straight ahead towards the enemy, taking heavy punishment from the arrows, crossbow bolts, cannon-balls and ballista missiles which showered down upon them from the eight huge Genoese carracks which formed a part of the French fleet. These large vessels possessed towering, castle-like poops from which the serried ranks of missile-men could rain down darts, stones and iron bolts on to the unprotected decks of the smaller English ships.

Despite the punishment, the English grimly persisted in their attempts to grapple, or ram the enemy, ship for ship. With the vessels firmly locked together the English archers, at point-blank range, fired furious hails of arrows until they had rid the enemy ships of the missile-men in the shrouds and fighting-tops or behind the bulwarks. Then, with a loud battle-cry, the armoured men-at-arms surged forward over the bulwarks, apprehensively glancing downwards at the ribbon of water that lay betweeen the ships and which held death for the man unlucky enough to fall into it. Once on the enemy decks, the battle was much the same as any other struggle between men-at-arms on land; it surged and ebbed to and fro until by sheer physical strength – for which they were pre-eminent at that period – the English either killed their opponents or pushed them into the sea. The fight lasted seven hours, during which the English lost as least twenty of their ships but were finally left masters of the sea with four of the huge carracks captured and one aground.

Much has been said throughout about the deadly effect of the English arrows, about their penetrative powers and their length of killing range; little has been mentioned of the treatment of the men who suffered these dreadful wounds – in fact, little is known of this facet of mediaeval warfare. One John Morstede appears to have been the English Surgeon-General in the reign of Henry V, who authorised him to press into the army as many of his brethren as he considered necessary for the expedition against France. Yet only one, the same John Morstede, landed there; and although he afterwards selected fifteen assistants, three of them served as archers under Sir John Erpingham at Agincourt, instead of dressing the wounded. Probably all did military duty of some kind and consequently were, in like manner, exposed to a soldier's fate. The wounded, therefore, had no assistance beyond nature and their own, or their comrades', exertions. On the English side they were certainly few, whilst those of the enemy, as we learn from details of the battles, perished without the slightest effort being made for their relief.

Sir John Smythe, a military writer of the sixteenth century, wrote: '. . . frequently heard French Captains and gentlemen report that they did think the English archers used to poison their arrow-heads; because of great numbers of the French nation that many times had been wounded or hurt with arrows, very few had escaped with their lives, by reason that their wounds did so impostume that they could not be cured. In such concerts they did greatly err, because in truth, these imposthumations proceeded of nothing else but the rust of the arrow-heads remaining rankling in their wounds; and therefore by the experience of our ancient enemies, not only the great but the small wounds of our arrows have been always found more dangerous and hard to be cured, than the fire of any shot unpoisoned. Besides all which, it is to be noted that horses in the field, being wounded or but slightly hurt with arrows, do presently fall yerking, flinging and leaping as if they were mad, through the great pain that upon every motion they do feel in their flesh, veins and sinews, by the shaking of the arrows with their barbed heads hanging in them. In such sort, as be it in squadron or troop, they do disorder one another, and never leave until they have cast their masters.'

A considered surgical opinion of today gives it that a man shot with an arrow in mediaeval warfare died almost inevitably; even by modern standards of surgery, the extraction of a barbed arrow is a delicate and possibly fatal operation. The book of 'Messire Ambroise Paré, Concilleur et Premier Chirugeon du Roi François 1er' (1515–47), who followed the armies of that monarch, treats extensively of the wounds peculiar to military men, especially those inflicted by arrows. In order that his professional brethren might more fully comprehend the method of cure, the precautions to be adopted, the incisions they might venture upon, and the use of the necessary instruments, he has delineated these, as well as many different kinds of arrows in use in his time, and particularly the form of their heads, a proper acquaintance with which has a great bearing on the treatment of their wounds. Among the arrows he has introduced, some had the head inserted into the stele (wooden shaft of the arrow), others had the stele itself entering the head. In either case, the point remained behind in the wound and rendered it extremely dangerous. Paré does not pretend to give the forms of every arrow used in his age, but only those which he himself had at various times extracted. Paré thus describes his mode of removing an arrow from the fleshy parts of the body:

'Si le fer estoit barblé ainsi, qui souvent est les flèches Angloises, et estoit à l'endroit d'un os, ou inséré dedans, ce qui souvient advient au profond de muscles de la cuisse, de bras, de jambes, ou d'autres parties de-quelles y auroit grande distance, lors ne le convient pusser, mais plutôt dilater la playe, en évitant les nerfs et grands vaisseaux, ainsi que fait le bon et expert chirurgien anatomique. Aussi faut appliquer un dilatatoire, cavé en sa partie intérieure, et faire en sorte, que l'on puisse prende les deux ailes du fer, puis avec le bec de Grüe le tenir ferme, et tirer les trois ensemble.'

'If the iron was thus barbed which is often the case with English arrows, and was situated in or near a bone, which often happens, in the depth of the muscles of the thigh, arms or legs or other parts which would be far removed, you must not push but rather dilate the wound, avoiding the nerves and vessels, as does the good and expert anatomical surgeon. Also one must apply a dilator [retractor?] to hold the wound open; do it in such a way that you can take the two wings of the barb with pinchers [forceps?]. Keep it firm and pull or draw the three together.'

Paré apparently underwent much suffering and personal inconvenience and was unable to confine his practice wholly within professional bounds. Speaking of a 'Sergeant of Chastellat' – one of his patients – he says: 'I performed towards him the office of physician, surgeon, apothecary and cook, dressing his dinner as well as his wounds until the time he was completely cured.' The doctor adds: '*Le Dieu le guerrisse toujours*,' so that we may infer that his patient's gratitude, for these accumulated benefits, did not evaporate with the causes which had elicited them.

A day such as Agincourt might have been expected to break the French love of obsolete tactics, to have changed their fanatical methods of horsemen or dismounted knights trying to break an English force by frontal attack, only to be driven back in utter rout by English archers. But the day of enlightenment had yet to dawn and more bloody defeats were to follow. Henry had gone, dying of dysentery in 1422; the English were now led by the Regent, John, Duke of Bedford. His chief lieutenant was the Earl of Salisbury, other English leaders being the Earl of Suffolk, Lord Scales, Sir John Fastolf and John, Lord Talbot. The French were now employing Scottish troops in their efforts to defeat the English invaders; a complete army of 6,500 under the Earl of Douglas, had landed in France during April of 1424 and were serving with the French, who were also raising mercenaries in Lombardy and elsewhere.

Early in 1424, the town of Ivry, thirty miles west of Paris, had been recaptured by the French in a sudden raid; in June, Bedford sent the Earl of Suffolk to retake the town. This was done without a lot of trouble but the garrison shut themselves up in the castle, and, on July 5th, agreed to surrender on August 14th if they had not been relieved by that date. The thoughts of both sides now turned constantly in the direction of Ivry; the one wishing to relieve, the other to secure the castle and bring the French to battle. But wishes were not good enough, certainly not enough to prevent Bedford from joining Suffolk before the castle on the 13th of August, a move which caused the garrison, as promised, to march out and surrender on the following day.

But the French had mounted a relieving force, who directed their steps towards Verneuil on the Arve when they discovered that the cross of St George was flying over the walls of Ivry. Verneuil was an old walled town with a small English garrison, unable to stand long against the large French army that came against it. It is reported that they gained possession of the place by sending heralds to declare that the English had been defeated, parading Scots troops tied to horses' tails to represent English prisoners before the walls of the old town. On hearing this, Bedford mustered all his available troops and marched towards the town. He had under his command some 8,000 or 9,000 men, or about half the numbers of the combined French and Scottish forces.

The English marched ten miles from Damville, emerging from the forest on to the plain of Verneuil to see the French drawn up in front of them, on the crest of a gentle slope. The Scots occupied the right of the position and the French the left; each division nominally in three lines but soon to become merged into one. The Earl of Buchan, Constable of France, had marched the force to this forming-up place; then he had resigned command to his father-in-law, the Earl of Douglas. As at Agincourt, the army was largely dismounted, except for the wings. On the right was a body of about 900 Lombard crossbowmen, all on horseback, and in armour; the left wing was covered by 1,000 mounted men-at-arms, completely mailed with lance, battle-axe and barbed horses. There were also some militia, peasant levies, in the ranks – raw, untrained, ill-armed troops.

The English marched down into the dip and up the very gentle slope towards the French, halting just outside missile range, where Bedford deployed his army parallel to, and on the same frontage as, the enemy. He closely followed his brother Henry's formation at Agincourt in that everyone was dismounted, the front was in two divisions, one commanded by himself and the other by Salisbury. The centre of each division was occupied by men-at-arms and the archers were positioned on the flanks of both divisions. There was also a reserve, consisting of about 2,000 archers, used as a baggage-guard, in a leaguer about three-quarters of a mile to the rear.

So, at about four o'clock on the afternoon of the 17th of August 1424 the two armies began slowly to advance towards each other. Bedford gave the traditional signal:

'Avaunt, banners!'

After kneeling down and reverently kissing the ground, the troops responded:

'St George! Bedford!'

It was a great shout and, as always, it struck alarm in the French hearts.

As usual, each archer carried his double-pointed stake which he attempted to plant in the ground at about 250 yards' distance from the enemy. But the ground was hard so that the stakes would not plant easily and much time was wasted in trying to force them into the sunbaked earth; more time was consumed in passing the stakes forward from hand to hand until they reached the front rank. Before the hedge of stakes was half completed, the left-flank body of French mailed horse charged the archers and smashed through their ranks, forcing a passage over and through the half-erected stakes. The survivors of the ridden-down archers gathered together, forming a close-knit body for mutual protection, but the horsemen did not delay to deal with them, surging on towards the baggage-leaguer.

Bedford's men-at-arms moved steadily forward, although their right flank had been exposed, to come into close contact with the French men-at-arms of Comte d'Aumale's division with whom they clashed in fierce combat. It was claimed by men who had fought at both places that the hour-long struggle that took place at this point was fiercer than Agincourt; the English, outnumbered two to one, gradually forced their opponents back. Bedford was prominent in this mêlée, wielding his two-handed axe vigorously all around him, having dismounted from the bay charger that had carried him to the battle.

Salisbury's division encountered an even stiffer resistance from the Scots, who resolutely battled with sword, mace and battle-axe in the closest conflict for more than an hour, refusing to be dismayed even when their French allies on their left broke and fled from the field. The mounted Lombard crossbowmen on the right flank of the French army, driven wide by the fire of Salisbury's flank archers, rode around the English left and attacked the baggage-leaguer. The baggage-guard being fiercely engaged with the French mailed cavalry of the other wing, the Lombards were at first completely successful, cutting down the poorly armed pages and varlets who tried valiantly to defend themselves and their wagons. Then the archers, who had completely routed the French mailed cavalry, came rushing across to fight off the Lombards, who, in their turn, were driven helter-skelter from the field. Having amazingly disposed of both bodies of cavalry, the exhilarated English archers sought fresh fields to conquer; they saw the battle still raging on the left front and determined to take a hand in it. Forming up, they wheeled in a headlong charge into the exposed right flank of the sorely tried Scottish division, uttering their fearsome shout as they came.

Under this new blow, the Scots reeled; but more was to come. Bedford's men-at-arms, having exhaustedly pursued the fleeing French men-at-arms as far as the town ditch, were now re-formed and doggedly, if wearily, trudged their heavily armoured way back into the fight – no mean feat in the heat of a summer's day. They struck into the rear of the Scots, who were now being hacked relentlessly down until hardly a man remained. In fact, the Scottish army ceased to exist. In addition to at least fifty Scottish gentlemen of rank who died, there fell the Constable of France, Buchan; his father-in-law, the venerable Earl of Douglas, who had already lost an eye at Homildon Hill; Hop-Pringle of Swailholm, Sir Robert Stewart, Sir John Swinton, Sir Alexander Home, two Sir James Douglases and Sir Walter Lindsay. The French lost most of their leaders who stayed and fought when deserted by the rank-and-file – Aumale, the commander, Narbonne, Ventadour, Tonnerre, the Lords Graville and Rambouillet and many knights from Languedoc and Dauphiné. Five thousand men, at least, fell; most of them Scots. Many were wounded, among them the Duc d'Alencon and the Marshal Lafayette, who became two of the few prisoners taken on this bloody day. The English loss was also heavy, but the figure of 1,000 casualties was worthwhile, for this 'Second Agincourt' left the French disheartened, dispersed and without leaders.

The war dragged on, with the English continuing their victorious way. In 1428 John, Duke of Bedford, the Regent, was still in command and committed the army to lay siege to Orléans; an affair largely consisting of desultory artillery fire, interspersed with occasional sorties and sallies, it dragged wearily on through the winter. Early in February, with Lent approaching and a staple diet of fish required, it was decided to send from Paris a big convoy of salted herrings to the besiegers. Under the command of Sir John Fastolf, a name made familiar, under another spelling, by Shakespeare, the convoy was made up of about 300 wagons, with an escort of 1,000 mounted archers in addition to wagoners and grooms.

News of this convoy reached the French; the Comte de Clermont marched north-east to intercept it on the Orléans road. He had under his command about 3,000 men, including a contingent of Scots under Sir John Stewart of Darnley, who was Constable of the Scots in France; also present were the lances of the Comte de Dunois. Clermont also had with him a large number of small-calibre cannon.

The convoy spent the night of the 11th of February in the small village of Rouvray, being on the point of resuming their march next morning when patrols came in with news of the approaching French force. Old soldier Fastolf immediately realised that his cumbersome wagons in their three-mile-long convoy were impossible to protect adequately with his small force, particularly against superior numbers of mounted enemy. About a mile outside the village the road ran along the top of a small ridge, giving an unimpeded view in all directions. Here Fastolf hastily formed his wagons into a protective leaguer, very similar to those formed centuries later by Western pioneers against the attacks of Indians.

Clermont came up with the convoy at seven in the morning, first appearing on the south-west skyline in a glittering of armour and a forest of lance-points. He was surprised to find himself confronted with this novel hedgehog inside which the English had retired. But, in spite of being some 450 years earlier, Clermont had something that the Indians did not possess – he had artillery! Cleverly he fitted his tactics to suit the situation; instead of making a direct attack on the leaguer, he ordered an artillery bombardment. To this attack the English had no reply and were forced to sit tight and take it; casualties mounted and herrings spilled on the road from split barrels. It seemed as though, for the first time in military history, guns alone were going to bring victory in the field, ushering in a new era of a vastness beyond fifteenth-century man's comprehension.

However, the march of progress was to be thwarted by the characteristic impetuosity of the Scottish contingent, eager to avenge the day of Verneuil. Their leader, Stewart of Darnley, contrary to Clermont's orders, dismounted his men, who advanced prematurely and impulsively to attack the barricade with sword and battle-axe, suffering greatly from the hail of English arrows that greeted their advance. Seeing that the Scots were wavering, Clermont was forced to support them by an attack of mounted men-at-arms, only to see it break down on the archers' pointed stakes, just as similar attacks had done so often in the past. Both Scots and French turned and retreated back to their starting-point, heads bowed against the showers of arrows that saw them off. Clermont resigned himself to resuming the artillery bombardment.

But it was not to be; Fastolf saw that the time had come for the counter-attack. Mounting his men, he sent two columns of cavalry pouring from the twin openings in the leaguer, to fall upon the already shaken enemy. The conflict was short but sharp, and the Franco-Scottish force were soon routed and fleeing from the field, leaving Stewart of Darnley and one of his sons dead, Dunois wounded and 'six score of great lords and 500 men there fell.'

The battle ended, the villagers came out and regaled themselves on the salted herrings that lay in the road around the splintered barrels – to them it was not the Battle of Rouvray but the Day of the Herrings! It was not really a battle, but a small affair in which the English proved, as they had done in the greater fields of the past, that they were superior to the French in more ways than one. Not the least of these was the fact that the archers, the ordinary soldiers, were respected by the lords and knights who led them into battle. It was a very different situation from that prevailing in France, where the nobles arrogated to themselves alone the honour of bearing arms, despising the common soldier so that even in the fifteenth century French infantry were composed of the most wretched class of people. This was illsutrated in the manner in which they were charged and ridden down by their own lords and commanders on those occasions when some distinguished act had aroused jealousy or scorn. The French foot soldier had reason to feel that for him to exhibit any true military qualities was simply to imperil his own life.

PART FOUR

THE TIDE BEGINS TO TURN

19

Patay – 1429; and Formigny – 1450

The second quarter of the fifteenth century found France, for
the first time perhaps, really facing up to the fact that the old,
chivalrous methods of warfare paid no dividends; that some
effective innovation had to be discovered to combat the English
system. Through bitter necessity and hard experience, the professional officers of France – Xaintrailles, La Hire and Dunois,
for example – stumbled upon a method of minimising the superiority of the English archers. It was so simple that it had probably
been considered and discarded many times; in short, when the
English were found drawn up in a good defensive position, the
French refused to attack. For the first time the French admitted
to themselves that there was little or no chance of beating an
English army in such a position, then likewise there was no point
in thrusting forward large bodies of troops as a target to be riddled
with English arrows. The French commanders knew that the
longbow had the ability to keep heavier-armed men at a distance –
therein lay its superiority; but once the cavalry or men-at-arms
got among the archers and their supporting men-at-arms, weight
of numbers might well decide the resulting mêlée – and the
French could usually put more men into the field.

With this enlightenment came some French victories; the
usual tactical causes of the English defeats lay in the French
attacking them when they were on the march, in camp or in
towns where it was impossible quickly to form an order of battle
on ground specifically chosen for its defensive qualities. This
tendency towards a reversal in the almost monotonous run of
English victories inevitably led to a noticeable shedding of the
old confidence born of persistent success over men using futile
tactics. There was a little more caution displayed, initiative
became stifled and plans could not be made with the former
certainty of success. Both commanders and men in the English
armies were too experienced and professional in their outlook
for this new situation to drop their morale to too low a level;
but they were perturbed, almost indignant. Naturally, with

success and the knowledge that the English were not quite so sure of themselves, the French confidence swelled up enormously and they began to seek, and win, conflicts where they were able, in a sudden onslaught, to hit the English before they could form up defensively.

The English commanders, with the traditions of Crécy, Poitiers, Agincourt and a host of similar but smaller battles behind them, disliked taking the offensive. When the opposing commanders refused to attack them in their carefully chosen position where they stood deliberately prepared but held off until such time as they could assail when least expected, then the English began to lose battles. A situation began to arise where the English forces were always liable to a sudden onslaught – Patay, fought on the 18th of June 1429, is a fair example of the sort of conflict that now took place.

Patay occurred at a time when the French, inspired by Joan of Arc, had recently raised the siege of Orléans and were endeavouring to capture those Loire towns still in English hands. An English force under Lord John Talbot and Sir John Fastolf, numbering perhaps 3,000 men, were retreating towards Patay after an unsuccessful attack on the Loire bridge at Meung, eighteen miles south. Hot on their heels in pursuit were the mounted vanguard of the Duc d'Alençon, moving considerably faster than the English, who were regulated by the speed of their baggage-train. In their attempts to make contact with the English, Alençon had patrols scouting in all directions; the English had similar groups in their rear to warn them of the arrival of the enemy. The word eventually came – the French advance-guard was close on their heels; at about the same moment the French discovered the whereabouts of the English, who revealed their position by characteristically raucous 'Halloos!' as a stag burst through their ranks!

Halting at a point where their track diverged from the old Roman road over which they had been marching, the English looked in a hurry for a good defensive position. The country was dotted with small clumps of trees and hedges, some of which bordered the road and were ideal for lining with archers; in a slight dip in the ground, Talbot stood with about 500 men. Fastolf deployed the main body on a ridge south-east of Patay, about 200 yards behind Talbot.

Topping the slight rise, the mounted French advance-guard saw the English drawn up in the dip in front of them; the archers were hammering their stakes into the ground and preparing their bows. Composed of specially selected men, well mounted and led by La Hire and Poton de Xantrailles, two of the most experienced commanders in the French army, it was a force alight with fervour imparted to the whole army by the Maid of Orléans. Pausing only to take in the situation, the cavalry thundered down the slope in a wild torrent to burst upon the startled archers before a bow could be drawn upon them, hitting them frontally and in flank. The lightly armed infantry stood no chance whatsoever; they were overwhelmed in a matter of seconds and cut down where they stood, the few who did manage to scramble away only adding to the confusion and dismay that covered Fastolf's men on the ridge.

Well might they be dismayed; their deployment on the ridge had been slow and they were far from completing their formation. They were not a particularly well-trained or experienced bunch of men, besides being dispirited by the retreat from Meung. They were able to do practically nothing before the French were through Talbot's force and upon them. The situation was made even more grave by the rapid arrival of the French main body, right on the heels of their advance-guard. It was all over very quickly; Talbot and most of the other leaders were captured, but Fastolf managed to get away, leaving behind his baggage and guns.

His escape was a little epic in itself, consisting of marching sixty miles in a day and a night, formed up in a stout body of archers who fought off every attack with arrows and then, when they were all gone, taking to the sword before reaching safety. But their weary steps were dogged with confusion and bewilderment – never before had they experienced anything like the French cavalry's headlong charge; they found it difficult to fathom this dramatic transition from the usual French prudence tinged with apprehension.

It was a bewilderment that was to grow. For more than 100 years the tactical employment of the English archer had brought success and each battle can be said to have favourably influenced the battle that followed. Crécy had been won because of the experience gained at Halidon Hill; Agincourt was, in its turn, influenced by Crécy and Poitiers. Now the wheel was turning. The side that had always won were prevented from continuing their victorious path because their opponents no longer played the game to the heavily loaded English rules. And the wheel turned in another inverse manner – just as the French had been continuously beaten through a slavish adherence to outmoded tactics, now came an anomalous turn. English commanders were being defeated by the improved military skill of the French because they persisted in slavishly applying the defensive tactics of Edward III and Henry V. For more than a century the French had been desperately trying to discover a method or a tactic that would minimise the deadly longbow; now the English were forced to think hard. They had to come up with some new system as successful as the longbow to deal with the superior numbers of the French, otherwise the English were foredoomed to defeat by their numerical inferiority.

In 1450, on the 15th of April, the English lost the Battle of Formigny because their commanders were unintelligently influenced by the tactics of Agincourt, coupled with the fact that the French no longer made gross blunders at every engagement. It was the last battle but one to be fought in the Hundred Years War – a small-scale engagement, but one that decided the fate of all Normandy. At Caen the Duke of Somerset, commander of all the English armies in France, was threatened by an overwhelming force, led by King Charles of France in person. To open the way to him, an English army of about 4,000 men had been scraped together by stripping Norman fortresses of their garrisons and bringing some 2,500 reinforcements from England, under the command of Sir Thomas Kyriell. It was a force made up of a few hundred men-at-arms, about 1,500 archers and the remainder were billmen.

At first the force had some successes; by mid-April they had come to the area around the village of Formigny, where they found themselves confronted by a French corps under the young Count of Clermont. It was one of several French divisions that had been sent out to arrest the progress of the English force; it consisted of about 3,000 men, thus being numerically inferior to the English force. Nevertheless, the English commander refused to assume the initiative; he grouped his force in the little valley containing the village, with their backs to a small brook lined with orchards and plantations well calculated to cover their rear. The veteran English commander, experienced in the defensive battles that had previously brought success, forgot the need to push forward; he awaited Clermont's attack and made every preparation to defeat it when it came. His archers, with plenty of time at their disposal, planted their stakes, dug ditches and potholes in front of their line to impede the enemy cavalry – it was a throw-back of over a century. Kyriell formed his men up on a frontage of about 1,000 yards in a thin line of dismounted men-at-arms, with three groups of archers projecting forward in bastions; it was Henry V's formation at Agincourt thirty-five years before.

At about three o'clock in the afternoon, the French force came marching straight up the road; they deployed in three lines to the right and left so that they faced the English, who were about 500 yards away. There both sides stood, eyeing one another. The French noted with some apprehension that the English were still improving their already substantial defences. The French commanders went into conference – in the old days they would have rushed forward in a headlong attack, but the new-style French army did things differently. Actually, the young and inexperienced Clermont was all for the immediate attack – he burned with the impetuosity of youth. However, he was sufficiently malleable to listen to his more experienced officers, who warned him, through long experience, to be wary of the English in a prepared position. Anyway, why hurry? Was not the Constable de Richemont near at hand with reinforcements?

So, for two or three hours some aimless skirmishing went on; it was a period of far more use to the French than to the English, for their reinforcements drew nearer by the minute. Some French attacks, on foot, were put in to feel out the flanks, but all were repulsed, as were some half-hearted mounted attacks also on the flanks. From their position behind stakes and pot-holes, the archers took a heavy toll of the enemy. De Richemont still had not arrived when Clermont recalled that he had brought guns with him; he ordered Giraud, Master of the Royal Ordnance, to drag up his two culverins. Under the eyes of the possibly apprehensive English, willing hands dragged the heavy guns to a spot outside bow range from which they could enfilade the English line.

After the usual fussy, technical preparations beloved of gunners throughout the ages, they opened fire. It was a galling, nagging bombardment, shots regularly arriving in irritating succession until the archers were so frustrated that they broke their ranks and rushed out from behind their stakes. Aided by a wing of the billmen, they charged headlong at the guns and a fierce but brief mêlée took place around them until the French were routed and reeled away, leaving the precious pieces silent and in the hands of the English.

The battle would have been won had Kyriell advanced his whole force at this crucial moment. The French, dispirited by their losses, were beginning to melt away from the field and the archers were triumphantly trying to drag the heavy guns back to their own lines, not knowing how to 'spike' them. But the English commander, obsessed by his defensive tactics, would not move an inch; he did not even send out aid to the archers who had seized the guns but were themselves now under great pressure, having been attacked by one of the flank 'battles' of French dismounted men-at-arms. A desperate struggle was taking place around the artillery pieces, archers and billmen battling to hold off their attackers whilst others strained and sweated in their efforts to get the guns away. It was an uneven struggle; the more lightly armed English were slowly but remorselessly pushed back by their heavier opponents, whilst their comrades looked on sullenly a few hundred yards away. Eventually the English infantry had to abandon the guns altogether as they fought for their very lives.

The very resistance of the archers proved disastrous to the English in their strong position, because the French pushed them back before them in a slow and progressive advance towards the stakes, so that the archers were unable to use their bows to harass the enemy for fear of hitting their own men. Soon the fighting was taking place immediately in front of the stakes, and the rest of the French force, seeing the battle going their way, had moved forward all along their line so that fierce fighting was taking place at all points. But the English superiority in numbers began to tell, and the French were showing signs of wavering when de Richemont arrived on the skyline with his reinforcements. They came from a direction that immediately threatened the English left flank and rear.

Kyriell was now in dire straits; he had no reserve, so was forced to bend his line back into a right-angle, or rough semicircle, to fight on the two fronts. The arrival of the new troops brought heart to Clermont's weary men so that they found new strength; but the fatigued and discouraged English began to crumple under the shock. Fighting hard, they gave ground until they were forced into several fiercely fighting but isolated groups, which fought on stubbornly and died hard with no quarter being given or asked. One party of 500 archers are said to have fought to the very last man, in the bloody, muddy ground of a garden by the brookside. A few hundred archers escaped, but Kyriell and his infantry were surrounded and annihilated, the commander himself being spared and captured. Four-fifths of the English force were killed in this major disaster to the English arms. By the use of intelligent offensive tactics it was a battle that could have been won before it even began, and then won again halfway through its course.

PART FIVE

THE LAST VICTORIES

20

The Wars of the Roses – 1461

At the time of the expulsion of the English from their Continental possessions, no blame was laid at the door of the longbow, nor did there seem to be any permanent discrediting of its power. Nevertheless, as future events proved, in spite of the triple victories of Crécy, Poitiers and Agincourt, to say nothing of many lesser successes, archery as a weapon of war was on the downgrade in the mid-fifteenth century. The bow still retained its supremacy as a missile weapon over the clumsy arbalest, with its complicated array of wheels and levers. In fact, the testimony of all Europe was given in favour of the longbow – Charles of Burgundy considered a corps of 3,000 English bowmen to be the flower of his infantry; thirty years before, Charles of France had made the archer the basis of his new militia in a vain attempt to naturalise the weapon of his enemies beyond the Channel. After a similar endeavour, James of Scotland had resigned himself to ill success and so turned the archery of his subjects to ridicule. Before that, however, he had ordered a law to be passed by the Scottish Parliament in 1424:

'That all men might busk thame to be archares, fra they be 12 years of age; and that at ilk ten pounds worth of land, thair be made bow makres, and specialle near paroche kirks, quhairn upon hailie days men may cum, and at the leist schute thrusye ab out, and have usye of archarie; and whassa usis not archarie, the laird of the land sall rais of him a wedder, and giff the laird raisis not the same pane, the kings shiref or his ministers sall rais it to the King.'

In England Edward IV proclaimed that every Englishman and Irishman living in England must have of his own a bow of his own height 'to be made of yew, wych, or hazel, ash or auborne or any other reasonable tree, according to their power'. The same law provided that buttes or mounds of earth for use as marks must be erected in every town and village, and listed a series of penalties for those who did not practise with the longbow.

Richard III was one of the kings who recognised the value

of the archer; Shakespeare makes him say, just prior to the Battle of Bosworth: 'Draw archers, draw your arrows to the head!' There are also records telling that Richard sent a body of 1,000 archers to France to aid the Duke of Brittany. Henry VII also provided anti-crossbow legislation and sent large levies of English archers to fight for the Duke of Brittany. During this entire period English longbowmen served in many parts of the then-known world.

The introduction of gunpowder was the beginning of the end for the archer; although over 400 years were to pass before the bow and arrow were finally overcome by gun-fire, the seeds were sown in the fourteenth century at Crécy and Sluys. The making of a skilful archer was a matter of years, but an adequate gunner could be produced in a few months – it was far too easy to attain a certain amount of proficiency with the new weapons for the bow to remain highly popular. At first the longbow was vastly superior to the newly invented handguns and arquebuses, which did not attain any great degree of efficiency before the end of the fifteenth century. When they did, the bow – the weapon par excellence of England – fell into disuse, although the archer could discharge twelve or fifteen arrows while the musketeer was going through the lengthy operation of loading his piece. The longbow could be aimed more accurately and its effective range of 200 – 240 yards was greater; the hitting-power of a war-arrow, weighing about two ounces, was far greater than that of a musket-ball, weighing from one-third to half an ounce. Archers could be lined up as many as ten deep and shoot together over each other's heads to put down an almost impassable barrage; and it was a terrifying barrage that could be seen descending. It is not outside the bounds of possibility to claim that the musket used at Waterloo in 1815 was inferior to the longbow used at Agincourt in 1415, both in range and accuracy.

Early firearms were reasonably good weapons of defence when they could be rested upon ramparts and their powder kept dry, otherwise they were far less deadly than the longbow in competent hands. In 1590 Sir John Smyth, a formidable military writer of the time, in his work *The Discourse* presented a wholesale condemnation of the new weapons, the mosquet, the caliver and the harquebus. The book was hastily suppressed by English military authorities; the stern, lone voice, crying for a return to the older and more effective ways of the longbow did not coincide with current military thinking. One also had to consider that the merit of early firearms lay in the prestige which they brought to the princes who armed their men with them.

In many of the battles of the Wars of the Roses, artillery was combined with archers, so that the enemy was put in a position where he had either to fall back or to escape missile fire – just as similar tactics had won the field of Hastings for William in 1066. Edgecott Field was notable as a renewed attempt of spearmen to stand against a mixed force of archers and cavalry. Here the Yorkists were entirely destitute of light troops, their bowmen having been drawn off by their commander, Lord Stafford, in a fit of pique. This meant that Pembroke and his North Welsh troops were left unsupported. The natural result followed; in spite of the strong position of the King's son, the rebels, by force of archery fire, quickly caused them to descend from the hill into the valley, where they were ridden down by the Northern horse as they retreated in disorder.

During the period of this war, armour had possibly reached its elaborate peak, as an old description of a knight arming for the Battle of Tewkesbury indicated: '. . . and arming was an elaborate process then, as the knight began with his feet, and clothed himself upwards. He put on first, his sabatynes or steel clogs; secondly, the greaves or shin-pieces; thirdly, the cuisses, or thigh-pieces; fourthly, the breech of mail; fifthly, the tuillettes; sixthly, the breastplate; seventhly, the vambraces or arm-covers; eighthly, the rerebraces, for covering the remaining part of the arm to the shoulder; ninthly, the gauntlets; tenthly, the dagger was hung; eleventhly, the short sword; twelfthly, the surcoat was put on; thirteenthly, the helmet; fourteenthly, the long sword was assumed; and, fifteenthly, the pennoncel, which he carried in his left hand.'

Notwithstanding the undoubted strength of this array, the archer still appeared to achieve sufficient penetration with his shafts to be considered a worthwhile part of the forces.

At Towton, on Palm Sunday, March 29th, 1461, Lord Falconbridge, commanding part of the army of Edward IV, used his archers in an interesting tactical expedient which sufficed to decide the day when both armies were employing the same weapon. The snow, which was falling very heavily, was being blown by a strong wind from behind the Yorkists and into the faces of the Lancastrians; it rendered the opposing lines only partially visible to each other. Falconbridge ordered his archers to the front, to act more or less as skirmishers. It must be explained that two types of arrows were then in use – the flight arrow and the sheaf arrow; the former was lightly feathered, with a small head; the latter was high-feathered and shortly shafted with a large head. Flight arrows were shot at a great distance and, at proper elevation, could kill at 240 yards. Sheaf arrows were for closer fighting, requiring but a slight elevation, and were often shot at point-blank range.

The advancing archers had been carefully instructed to let fly a shower of sheaf arrows, with a greater elevation than usual, and then to fall back some paces and stand. Aided by the gale, the Yorkist arrows fell among the Lancastrian archers, who, perceiving that they were sheaf arrows and being misled by the blinding snow as to their opponents' exact distance from them, assumed that the enemy were within easy range. They commenced firing volley after volley into the snowstorm, all of which fell sixty yards short of the Yorkists until the snow bristled with the uselessly expended shafts like porcupine quills. When the Lancastrians had emptied their belts, the Yorkists moved forward and began firing in return, using not only their own shafts but also those so conveniently sticking out of the snow at their feet. Their shooting had great effect and men fell on all sides as the wind-assisted shafts came hissing into them; in a short time it was possible for the billmen and men-at-arms of Warwick and King Edward to advance comfortably forward without receiving any harassing fire from the Lancastrian archers. Needless to say, the Yorkist archers then laid aside their bows and went in with the more heavily armed infantry. It was a strategem that won the battle, and was one that could only be used when the adversaries were perfectly conversant with each other's armaments and methods of war.

Even in the late fifteenth and early sixteenth centuries the longbow still retained its supremacy over the arquebus and had yet some famous fields to win, notably that of Flodden in 1513, where, as will be seen from the next chapter, the old manoeuvres of Falkirk were repeated by both parties, the pikemen of the lowlands once again being shot to pieces by the archers of Cheshire and Lancashire. As late as the reign of Edward VI we find Kett's Insurgents beating, by the rapidity of their archery fire, a corps of German hackbuteers whom the government had sent against them. Nor was the bow entirely extinct as a national weapon even in the days of Queen Elizabeth. It was in the reign of the Virgin Queen that the first really great archery writer appeared on the English scene. Roger Ascham, tutor to Elizabeth when she was a princess, was the author of the book *Toxophilus*, which remains the classic in the field. Allowing for certain minor differences,

the phraseology and certain advances which have been made in
equipment, Ascham's book is as valuable to the archer today as
it was when it was written four centuries ago. His 'instructions'
can be, and are, used today in teaching novice archers. Ascham's
relation to the bow corresponds to that of Izaak Walton to the
rod and reel.

21

Flodden Field – 1513

The longbow was to go out of military fashion in a blaze of
glory, to achieve a victory in the old classical style so that it
left a glow in the hearts of the yeoman of England, but no pangs
of regret in the hearts of his enemies.

The events which led to the Scottish invasion of England in
1513 need not be recapitulated; suffice to say that King James IV
of Scotland had crossed the border in mid-August of that year
with, for that time, an enormous army of 40,000 men. They
were well furnished with the latest artillery of the day. His leaders
were all those of the highest rank in the Scottish kingdom; it may
be fairly said that no grown-up member of any family of position
was absent from the expedition. After some initial skirmishing,
the Scots had Northumberland at their mercy; but after taking the
castle of Ford, stronghold of the Heron family, James loitered
in the neighbourhood whilst his army daily grew less in numbers.
Said to have been infatuated by the captured Lady Heron, King
James appeared to be regardless of the increasing desertions of
those gorged with plunder in addition to those starved through
the land being foraged-out. Finally, his army numbered less than
30,000, but those that were left represented the cream of the whole
and were claimed to have been one of the noblest bodies of
fighting men ever gathered together. To back them, James had a
most efficient train of thirty pieces of artillery which had been
cast for him at Edinburgh by the master gunner, Robert Borthwick.

Against the Scots was sent the veteran Earl of Surrey, over
seventy years of age, and forced, on account of his rheumatism,
to travel mostly by coach. Chiefly from the northern counties,

he hastily gathered together an army of between 20,000 and 26,000 men. Whilst encamped at Alnwick, Surrey sent a formal challenge to King James, naming Friday, 9th September, as the day of battle; the challenge was duly accepted in the most formal manner. At the time of acceptance, James was encamped in the low ground and, according to the old rules of chivalry, his acceptance from this spot implied that he would give battle on that site. But before long James had moved his camp from there to Flodden Hill, an eminence lying due south of Ford Castle, running east and west in a low ridge. Here, on the steep brow of Flodden Edge, in the angle between the Till and its small tributary, the Glen, James's defensive position was so strong that no sane foe would dare to attack it.

Realising this, Surrey sent James a letter of reproach in which he pointed out that the arrangement had been made for a pitched battle, and instead James had installed himself in a fortified camp. He concluded by challenging him to come down on the appointed day and fight on Millfield Plain, a level tract south of Flodden Hill. King James refused even to see the herald who brought the message.

Surrey then marched his army up the river Till; put his vanguard with the artillery and heavy baggage across at the Twizel bridge, whilst the remainder of his force crossed at Sandyford, half a mile higher up. Now was presented to James an excellent opportunity of attacking the English whilst they were split into two parts. By failing to grasp it, James now found his foes placed between himself and Scotland; he was left with little alternative but to reverse his order of battle. Setting fire to the rude huts that his men had constructed on the summit of the hill, he moved his force on to Branxton Hill, immediately behind Flodden Edge; the movement was partially obscured from the English by the clouds of smoke that trailed over the brow of the hill. As they formed up on the ridge above Branxton, the Scottish army that had faced south were now drawn up facing north.

The two armies faced each other, both formed into four divisions and both with a reserve. Beginning on the English right, the first division was commanded by Sir Edmund Howard, the younger son of the Earl of Surrey; opposed to him were the Gordons under the Earl of Huntley and the men of the border under the Earl of Home. The second English division was led by Admiral Howard, who was faced by the Earls of Crawford and Montrose. The Earl of Surrey, with the third division, was opposed by King James himself; while Sir Edward Stanley, with the fourth division, had to try conclusions with the Earls of Lennox and Argyle, whose troops were mainly highlanders. The English reserve, mainly cavalry, was commaded by Lord Dacre; that of the Scottish under Bothwell.

It was not until four o'clock that the battle commenced. Then, as an old chronicler says: 'Out burst the ordnance with fire, flame and a hideous noise . . . .' The Scottish artillery was far superior in construction to the English, which was constructed of hoops and bars, whilst the Scots master gunner had cast his weapons; there were, however, more English guns. It seems as though the English gunners were superior to those serving the Scottish cannon, the latter committing the error of firing at too great an elevation so that their shots passed over the heads of the English and buried themselves in the marshy ground beyond. The old writer goes on to say: '. . . and the master gunner of the English slew the master gunner of the Scots, and beat all his men from their guns.' The early death of Borthwick, brought down by a ball, set up a panic in his men, who ran from their guns – but it was not so by artillery fire that Flodden was to be won or lost. James realised this fact and ordered an attack; the border troops of the Lords Huntley and Home appear to have been the first to come to close quarters with the English.

In an unusual silence the Scots rushed forward, their twelve-foot-long pikes levelled in front of them; the initial impetus of their onslaught carried them far into the English lines, so that at first they achieved absolute success. The English right, under Sir Edmund Howard, was thrust back, their leader thrice beaten down and his banner overturned. The English fighting line was in disorder on this flank. Some Cheshire archers, who had been separated from their corps and sent out to strengthen the right wing, fled in all directions and chaos came to Howard's wing. John Heron, usually known as the Bastard Heron, at the head of a group of Northumbrians, checked the rout long enough for Dacre to charge down with his reserve. This committing of the reserve at such an early stage did not succeed in restoring the English line, but it did put Huntley to flight, whilst the undisciplined borderers of Home had no further idea of fighting. In a border foray, no more was expected after routing one's opponents; Home's men did not grasp that Flodden was no ordinary foray – 'We have fought and won, let the rest do their part as well as we!' was their answer to those trying to rally them.

Whilst this was going on, Crawford and Montrose were furiously attacking the division of Admiral Howard; so much so that the Admiral sent to his father, the Earl of Surrey, for assistance. But Surrey was fully occupied in holding his own against the division commanded by King James, strengthened by Bothwell, who had brought up the reserve and flung them into the struggle. The battle was now at its height and was being hardily contested all along the line; it seemed, here and there, as though the English halberds were proving more deadly weapons at close quarters than the long Scottish pikes.

On the English left, the archers of Cheshire and Lancashire, under Sir William Molyneaux and Sir Henry Kickley, were pouring volleys of arrows into the tightly packed ranks of the Scottish right, highlanders under the Earls of Lennox and Argyle. Galled by the hail of shafts which spitted their unarmoured bodies, the wild clansmen finally found it to be more than they could bear. Casting aside their targets and uttering wild, fierce yells, they flung themselves forward in a headlong rush, claymore and pole-axe waving furiously in a frenzy of anxiety to bury themselves into English flesh and bone. The bowmen and pikemen were shaken, so tremendous was the initial shock, their bills and swords, which had replaced the bows, reeling and wavering under the onslaught; but discipline prevailed and their formation remained unbroken. The archers on the flanks of the mêlée stood back and poured in volley after volley at close quarters, while the inner line of pikemen and men-at-arms held off the wild highlanders. Their arrows gone, the archers threw down their bows, drew their swords and axes to fling themselves into the fray, both in front and on the flanks. It was a deadly struggle whilst it lasted, but gradually the clansmen gave way, fighting at first, but then, suddenly, in complete rout – both earls died trying to stem the tide.

Stanley pressed forward, won his way up and crowned the ridge. He did not make the error of pursuing from the field the thoroughly broken Scots whom his men had just beaten. Facing about, he charged obliquely downhill to take the Scots divisions of King James and Bothwell in flank. This struggle in the centre, between Surrey and King James, had been proceeding fiercely; the King was fighting on foot like the rest of his division, conspicuous by the richness of his arms and armour. Stanley's flank attack, coinciding with a similar attack on the other flank by Dacre and Edmund Howard, proved disastrous to the Scots. Hemmed in on all sides, they began to fall by hundreds in the close and deadly mêlée; no quarter was asked by either side and none was given. The blood flowing from the dreadful gashes inflicted by axes, bills and two-handed swords made the ground so slippery that many of the combatants were said to have taken off their boots to gain a surer footing.

As a battle, all was over by now and nothing remained but the slaughter. Surrounded by a solid ring of his knights, James refused to yield until he finally fell, dying with the knights who had formed a human shield around him. He was said to have been mortally wounded by a ball fired by an unknown hand; he had several arrows in his body, a gash in his neck and his left hand was almost severed from his arm. Ten thousand men fell on the Scottish side; to list the slain is almost to catalogue the ancient Scottish nobility. With the exception of the heads of families who were too old or too young to fight, there was hardly a family of top rank that did not grievously suffer. The English lost about 5,000 men.

On the Scots side, the archers of Ettrick, known in Scotland as the 'Flowers of the Forest', perished almost to a man. To this day the sweet, sad, wailing air known by that name is invariably the Dead March used by Scottish regiments.

22

The End of the Road

Except possibly in a great clan battle in 1688, when Macintosh fought Macdonald, the last occasion on which the longbow was used for war in Britain is said to have been at Tippermuir in 1644. Here the Marquis of Montrose, upholding the cause of Charles I, routed the Covenanters; his army, having little ammunition for their few muskets, used hails of stones and ancient bows to bring them victory. Since there were so many more battles during the next few years of that unhappy period, it is quite likely that the bow was used to good effect on other occasions – it seems unlikely that it should have been completely abandoned in the middle of a civil war. In 1622 the longbow was no longer mentioned in the list of weapons with which the military forces were to be armed.

One of the great puzzles of military history is why artillery and firearms replaced the longbow so rapidly when the latter, right up to the time of Waterloo and beyond, was capable of far greater range, rate of fire, and accuracy. In 1625, in his pamphlet *Double-armed Man*, W. Neade gave the effective range of the bow as sixteen to twenty score yards and claimed that the archer could discharge six arrows while the musketeer loaded and fired but once. In 1792 Lieutenant-Colonel Lee, of the 44th Regiment, strongly advocated the use of the longbow in preference to the flint-lock musket. To support his case he gave the following reasons:

1. Because a man may shoot as truly with the bow as with the common musket.

2. He can discharge four arrows in the time of charging and discharging one bullet

3. His object is not taken from his view by the smoke of his own side.

4. A flight of arrows coming upon them terrifies and disturbs the enemy's attention to his business.

5. An arrow sticking in any part of a man puts him *hors de combat* until it is extracted.

6. Bows and arrows are more easily made anywhere than muskets and ammunition.

As late as 1846 the effective range of the musket in common use in the British army was, for all practical purposes, only 100 to 150 yards – the common dictum being not to fire until you could see the whites of the enemy's eyes! Why then was the bow abandoned so early in favour of the crude firearms of the period?

On the battlefield, archery has certain unavoidable drawbacks affecting both the man and his weapon. To use his longbow effectively, the archer needed space around him – he had to stand to deliver his shaft. Not only did this make him vulnerable to the elements, it also turned him into a good target; the whole course of warfare was altered when the breech-loading rifle enabled the soldier to re-load his arm whilst lying down. Although rain had an adverse effect upon the rate of fire of a musket, it completely rendered the longbow useless; wind could also render the archer helpless. However, the crucial factor was that the archer had to be an athlete in the best physical condition, whereas the man behind the gun could function even in the state of weary debility produced by the cold, wet and hunger of extended active service. Mediaeval commanders were well aware of the importance of maintaining both the health and the stature of their archers – they mounted them on horses whenever possible, recruited them from the fixed heraldic rank of yeoman (the highest held by men of low degree) and ever encouraged practice at the butts.

Although the longbow won Crécy, Poitiers and Agincourt, together with a host of smaller engagements, the Hundred Years War was won by the French. By better adapting themselves to the newly invented and primitive artillery and by using them with a superior technique, the French were able to recapture the towns and provinces lost to the English, eventually nullifying the effects of all the English victories throughout the Hundred Years War.

Perhaps regrettably, today it is only the incurable romanticist who will claim special virtues for the longbow as against firearms. But, in the end, he will have grudgingly to admit that the firearm has proved to be what the bow could not become – a perfectible weapon. Any good shot in an average modern small-bore rifle club can get a 'possible' out of every ten shots aimed at a two-inch circle 100 yards away; he will be able to do this consistently and without hesitation. The 'gold' of an archery target is as big as a saucer, yet Horace A. Ford held for years the record of 28 hits in 75 shots at 60 yards. No archer, however skilful, can be absolutely certain within several inches where a single shaft will land. It is a degree of uncertainty emphasised by an incident at the inauguration of the National Rifle Association at Wimbledon on July 2nd, 1860, when Queen Victoria pulled a silken cord which fired a Whitworth rifle on a fixed rest and hit only $1\frac{1}{4}$ inches from the centre of the target!

Epilogue

In 1939 Captain Jack Churchill of the Manchester Regiment was a member of the British team competing in the World Archery Championship at Oslo. With war in the offing, the party arrived back in England after some difficulties and he went, almost immediately, with the advance party of the British Expeditionary Force to the Continent. Before embarking, Captain Churchill had made by Purle of London a hundred-pound yew bow together with hunting arrows; he also equipped himself with two steel bows which were later broken whilst sticking out of the back of a lorry that was backed against a wall.

During the days of the 'phoney war' of 1939, Captain Churchill took every opportunity of practising with his bow by shooting at targets. In December 1939 the 4th Brigade of the 2nd Division of the B.E.F., consisting of the Norfolk Regiment, the Royal Scots, the Warwickshire Regiment, and the machine-guns of the Manchester Regiment, took over part of the Maginot line. It was a bitterly cold winter and snow lay on the frozen ground, so that patrols formed of groups from all battalions were sent out in front of the Maginot Line wearing white nightgowns and with elephantine legs encased in layers of straw and sandbags. Frustrated and irritated by the official policy of not provoking the enemy, Captain Churchill decided upon a symbolic gesture which he thought would not only give him great personal satisfaction but might also create a certain alarm, despondency and bewilderment in the enemy lines. On the 31st of December 1939, whilst out with a patrol amid the undulating, snow-covered countryside of no-man's-land, he stealthily made his way to between fifty and eighty yards from the German lines and, drawing his bowstring back to his cheek, let loose an arrow which he heard bite into a frost-hard ground with an audible 'clack'. There was no reaction whatsoever, so Churchill again drew his bow and loosed a second arrow – this time a German voice called out and there was obviously some consternation caused in the enemy defences, although he did not have the satisfaction of knowing whether or not his arrow had hit anyone. Although elated by his gesture, the archer regretted not being able to retrieve his arrows. The shafts cost him 10s. 6d. each and the War Office had no financial responsibility for such ammunition!

On the 27th of May 1940, whilst in command of a mixed force holding the village of L'Epinette, near Bethune, during the retreat to Dunkirk, Captain Churchill, who had been slightly wounded on the 25th, became the only European for centuries who, in the action of war, had killed an enemy with the longbow. Climbing into the loft of a small granary, through a vertical opening in one wall, normally used for hauling up sacks of grain, he saw, some thirty yards away, five German soldiers sheltering behind the wall but in clear view of the granary. Quickly and quietly Captain Churchill fetched up two infantrymen and instructed them to open rapid fire on the enemy but not to pull the trigger until he had loosed an arrow at the centre man. Captain Churchill lifted his bow, took careful aim and loosed the shaft. At the same time as the bow string twanged, the air was shattered by the rapid fire of the two infantrymen. Captain Churchill was delighted to see his arrow strike the centre German in the left of the chest and penetrate his body; the remaining Germans of the party slumped to the dusty ground. With the idea of retrieving his arrow by pushing or pulling it through the wound, Captain Churchill swiftly ran to the body but was unable to extract the shaft. In his haste he broke the arrow, leaving its barbed head in the German's body. At this moment enemy machine-gun fire was opened down the line of the road and everyone dived for cover.

Sheet 21 of the War Diary of the 4th Infantry Brigade, dated the 30th of May 1940, bears the following paragraph:

'One of the most reassuring sights of the embarkation was the sight of Captain Churchill passing down the beach with his bows and arrows! His actions in the Saar with his arrows are known to many and his disappointment at not having had the chance to keep in practice had tried him sorely. His high example and his great work with his machine-guns were a great help to the 4th Infantry Brigade.'

Five years before the first atomic bomb exploded and nearly 600 years after the Battle of Crécy an English archer had incongruously and briefly returned to the ancient battlefields of France.

NEL BESTSELLERS

Crime

T013 332	CLOUDS OF WITNESS	*Dorothy L. Sayers* 40p
T016 307	THE UNPLEASANTNESS AT THE BELLONA CLUB	*Dorothy L. Sayers* 40p
W003 011	GAUDY NIGHT	*Dorothy L. Sayers* 40p
T010 457	THE NINE TAILORS	*Dorothy L. Sayers* 35p
T012 484	FIVE RED HERRINGS	*Dorothy L. Sayers* 40p
T015 556	MURDER MUST ADVERTISE	*Dorothy L. Sayers* 40p

Fiction

W002 775	HATTER'S CASTLE	*A. J. Cronin* 60p
T013 944	CRUSADER'S TOMB	*A. J. Cronin* 60p
T013 936	THE JUDAS TREE	*A. J. Cronin* 50p
T001 288	THE TROUBLE WITH LAZY ETHEL	*Ernest K. Gann* 30p
T003 922	IN THE COMPANY OF EAGLES	*Ernest K. Gann* 30p
W002 145	THE NINTH DIRECTIVE	*Adam Hall* 25p
T012 271	THE WARSAW DOCUMENT	*Adam Hall* 40p
T012 778	QUEEN IN DANGER	*Adam Hall* 30p
T007 243	SYLVIA SCARLETT	*Compton Mackenzie* 30p
T007 669	SYLVIA AND ARTHUR	*Compton Mackenzie* 30p
T007 677	SYLVIA AND MICHAEL	*Compton Mackenzie* 35p
T009 084	SIR, YOU BASTARD	*G. F. Newman* 30p
T009 769	THE HARRAD EXPERIMENT	*Robert H. Rimmer* 40p
T010 252	THE REBELLION OF YALE MARRATT	*Robert H. Rimmer* 40p
T013 820	THE DREAM MERCHANTS	*Harold Robbins* 75p
T012 255	THE CARPETBAGGERS	*Harold Robbins* 80p
T016 560	WHERE LOVE HAS GONE	*Harold Robbins* 75p
T013 707	THE ADVENTURERS	*Harold Robbins* 80p
T006 743	THE INHERITORS	*Harold Robbins* 60p
T009 467	STILETTO	*Harold Robbins* 30p
T015 289	NEVER LEAVE ME	*Harold Robbins* 40p
T016 579	NEVER LOVE A STRANGER	*Harold Robbins* 75p
T011 798	A STONE FOR DANNY FISHER	*Harold Robbins* 60p
T015 874	79 PARK AVENUE	*Harold Robbins* 60p
T011 461	THE BETSY	*Harold Robbins* 75p
T010 201	RICH MAN, POOR MAN	*Irwin Shaw* 80p
W002 186	THE PLOT	*Irving Wallace* 75p
T009 718	THE THREE SIRENS	*Irving Wallace* 75p
T010 341	THE PRIZE	*Irving Wallace* 80p

Historical

T009 750	THE WARWICK HEIRESS	*Margaret Abbey* 30p
T013 731	KNIGHT WITH ARMOUR	*Alfred Duggan* 40p
T013 758	THE LADY FOR RANSOM	*Alfred Duggan* 40p
T011 585	THE ROSE IN SPRING	*Eleanor Fairburn* 30p
T009 734	RICHMOND AND ELIZABETH	*Brenda Honeyman* 30p
T011 593	HARRY THE KING	*Brenda Honeyman* 35p
T009 742	THE ROSE BOTH RED AND WHITE	*Betty King* 30p
T010 988	BRIDE OF LIBERTY	*Frank Yerby* 30p
T014 649	FAIROAKS	*Frank Yerby* 50p
T014 045	TREASURE OF PLEASANT VALLEY	*Frank Yerby* 35p

Science Fiction

T011 410	EARTHWORKS	*Brian Aldiss* 25p
T014 576	THE INTERPRETER	*Brian Aldiss* 30p
T014 347	SPACE RANGER	*Isaac Asimov* 30p
T016 900	STRANGER IN A STRANGE LAND	*Robert Heinlein* 75p
W002 908	STAR BEAST	*Robert Heinlein* 30p
T011 534	I WILL FEAR NO EVIL	*Robert Heinlein* 75p
W002 684	THE HEAVEN MAKERS	*Frank Herbert* 30p
T011 844	DUNE	*Frank Herbert* 75p

T012 298	DUNE MESSIAH	Frank Herbert	40p
T012 859	QUEST FOR THE FUTURE	A. E. Van Vogt	35p
T015 270	THE WEAPON MAKERS	A. E. Van Vogt	30p

War

T012 964	COLDITZ: THE GERMAN STORY	Reinhold Eggers	40p
T009 890	THE K BOATS	Don Everitt	30p
T013 324	THE GOOD SHEPHERD	C. S. Forester	35p
W002 484	THE FLEET THAT HAD TO DIE	Richard Hough	25p
W002 805	HUNTING OF FORCE Z	Richard Hough	30p
T012 999	P.Q. 17 – CONVOY TO HELL	Lund & Ludlam	30p
T011 755	TRAWLERS GO TO WAR	Lund & Ludlam	40p
T010 872	BLACK SATURDAY	Alexander McKee	30p
T010 074	THE GREEN BERET	Hilary St. George Saunders	40p
T010 066	THE RED BERET	Hilary St. George Saunders	40p

Western

T016 994	EDGE: No. 1: THE LONER	George Gilman	30p
T016 986	EDGE: No. 2: TEN THOUSAND DOLLARS AMERICAN	George Gilman	30p
T010 929	EDGE: No. 3: APACHE DEATH	George Gilman	25p
T017 001	EDGE: No. 4: KILLER'S BREED	George Gilman	30p
T016 536	EDGE: No. 5: BLOOD ON SILVER	George Gilman	30p
T013 774	EDGE: No. 6: THE BLUE, THE GREY AND THE RED	George Gilman	25p

General

T011 763	SEX MANNERS FOR MEN	Robert Chartham	30p
W002 531	SEX MANNERS FOR ADVANCED LOVERS	Robert Chartham	30p
W002 835	SEX AND THE OVER FORTIES	Robert Chartham	30p
T010 732	THE SENSUOUS COUPLE	Dr. 'C'	25p
P002 367	AN ABZ OF LOVE	Inge and Stem Hegeler	60p
P011 402	A HAPPIER SEX LIFE	Dr. Sha Kokken	70p
W002 584	SEX MANNERS FOR SINGLE GIRLS	Georges Valensin	25p
W002 592	THE FRENCH ART OF SEX MANNERS	Georges Valensin	25p
W002 726	THE POWER TO LOVE	E. W. Hirsch M.D.	47½p

Mad

S004 708	VIVA MAD!	30p
S004 676	MAD'S DON MARTIN COMES ON STRONG	30p
S004 816	MAD'S DAVE BERG LOOKS AT SICK WORLD	30p
S005 078	MADVERTISING	30p
S004 987	MAD SNAPPY ANSWERS TO STUPID QUESTIONS	30p

NEL P.O. BOX 11, FALMOUTH, CORNWALL

Please send cheque or postal order. Allow 6p per book to cover postage and packing.

Name ....

Address ....

....

Title ....

(APRIL)